Desperate Clarity

Desperate Clarity

CHRONICLES OF INTELLECTUAL LIFE, 1942

MAURICE BLANCHOT

Translated by Michael Holland

FORDHAM UNIVERSITY PRESS

New York   2014

The essays in this volume were published in French in *Chroniques littéraires du «Journal des débats»: Avril 1941–août 1944*, © Éditions Gallimard, Paris, 2007.

Cet ouvrage publié dans le cadre du programme d'aide à la publication bénéficie du soutien du Ministère des Affaires Etrangères et du Service Culturel de l'Ambassade de France représenté aux Etats-Unis.

This work received support from the French Ministry of Foreign Affairs and the Cultural Services of the French Embassy in the United States through their publishing assistance program.

Cet ouvrage a bénéficié du soutien des Programmes d'aide à la publication de l'Institut Français.

This work, published as part of a program of aid for publication, received support from the Institut Français.

Library of Congress Cataloging-in-Publication Data

Blanchot, Maurice.
  [Essays. Selections. English]
  Desperate Clarity : Chronicles of Intellectual Life, 1942 / Maurice Blanchot ; translated by Michael Holland.—First edition.
    pages   cm
  Includes bibliographical references and index.
  ISBN 978-0-8232-5099-8 (cloth : alk. paper)
  ISBN 978-0-8232-5100-1 (pbk. : alk. paper)
  1. Blanchot, Maurice—Criticism and interpretation.   2. Literature—Philosophy.
I. Holland, Michael, 1950– translator.   II. Title.
PQ2603.L3343A2   2014
843'.912—dc23

                                                          2013025575

Printed in the United States of America
16 15 14   5 4 3 2 1
First edition

Contents

Desperate Clarity

Introduction

MICHAEL HOLLAND

However vehemently Maurice Blanchot may have denounced the influence of circumstances and events on writers and their output after June 1940,[1] by the beginning of 1942 the harsh reality of defeat and occupation had become difficult to ignore. Indeed, events had begun to take a cruel turn well before then. The first executions of Resistance activists (the Musée de l'Homme group) were carried as early as February 1941. Jean Paulhan, who had been involved in their activities, was arrested, and it was only thanks to Drieu la Rochelle's intervention that he was freed. Friendship could clearly still prove stronger than politics. On August 21, Pierre George, who was later known as Colonel Fabien, carried out the first attack on a member of the occupying forces. In response, Vichy executed three members of the Communist party. In October, following two separate attacks on German officers in Bordeaux and Nantes, the Germans executed almost one hundred hostages.

On another front, March 1941 saw the establishment of the Commissariat Général aux Questions Juives, which was designed to give force and focus to the gradual build-up of anti-Semitic legislation on the part of the Vichy regime from the very first days of its existence. In September 1941 an exhibition entitled "Le Juif et la France" opened in Paris, and by the time it closed in January 1942, 200,000 people had visited it. In May 1941 the first arrests of foreign Jews took place and in August, an internment camp for both French and foreign Jews was opened in Drancy.[2] By early 1942 the Nazis had drawn up their plans for the Final Solution, and in March 1942 the first convoy of Jewish deportees left France for Auschwitz. In May, Jews in the nonoccupied zone were obliged to wear the yellow star of David, and on July 16 and 17, what was called "le rafle du Vél-d'Hiv" took place in Paris. On this occasion, nearly 13,000 Jews were rounded up and confined in a large sports arena before being transported to Drancy and then on to Auschwitz. Between March and December 1942, a total of 43,000 Jews were rounded up and deported.

In the harsh light of these developments, the fact that Blanchot's weekly chronicles appear to take no account of them becomes glaringly apparent. However clear it is by 1942 that something called *literature* is providing his only preoccupation and the sole measure of human affairs, it is hard to see what *value* that literary ideal could lay claim to, let alone the writing in which Blanchot so resolutely defends it. What interest could the situation of the nineteenth-century poet Lamartine[3] possibly hold, when the situation of so many living people had become an unimaginable horror simply because they were Jews? Could "Terror in literature"[4] be of any import when terror and counterterror were pitting French patriots against the German occupiers in a viciously unequal struggle?

The questions raised by Blanchot's literary activity in these years do not allow for easy answers. Of course, he was far from alone in appearing indifferent to events, and those questions make sense fully only if they are applied to all of the journalism, indeed all the writing and publishing which did not directly oppose Vichy and the Germans during the Occupation.[5] And if we were content to rank Blanchot along with the likes of Thierry Maulnier, his close associate during the 1930s, it would be relatively simple to close the book on his wartime writing and consider that, on balance, his reputation comes out intact.[6] The fact is, however, that we only read what Maurice Blanchot wrote before and during the war because of the name he made for himself in the postwar era. And the intellectual figure he has become today makes it impossible simply to draw a veil over what he wrote during the Occupation. Blanchot offered so many of his contemporaries a new approach to what is absolute that it is impossible to be content with such a partial and relative assessment of his significance. Put bluntly, we expect better from him than that.

Blanchot had left Clermont-Ferrand where the *Débats* were published shortly after the armistice and returned to Paris, where he became the literary director of Jeune France for the Occupied Zone. There he remained for the duration of the war, seeing the Jeune France venture through to the bitter end,[7] allowing himself to be drawn into Jean Paulhan's maneuvers to keep Drieu's *NRF* alive[8] and pursuing his friendship with Georges Bataille in mutually congenial circles. His second novel, *Aminadab*, came out in the autumn of 1942,[9] and the three separate articles he devoted to Paulhan's *Fleurs de Tarbes* in the *Débats* appeared as a slim volume with José Corti in February with the title *How Is Literature Possible?*[10]

As Blanchot continued to send his weekly chronicle to the *Débats* "by special channels,"[11] the rigid division of France into two zones placed a curious distance between his day-to-day existence and his appearance in print, setting up a strange ventriloquism whereby his voice was projected entirely beyond the hearing of those around him, while he remained a disembodied presence in the newsroom he had frequented for so long. The division went deeper than this, however. For the voice that, since 1937, had stridently spoken out for literature itself considered as the purest expression of French civilization, and that in 1941 could still intone that theme, even if only silently,[12] is becoming estranged from its impassioned espousal of France. The idyll is now riven by conflict. The ideal that it celebrated can no longer be framed as a union between literature and nation, because with the defeat of France the nation has ceased to exist except as a dividing line separating two false versions of itself. And what remains of the ideal is now exposed as a site of increasingly radical difference. It is not that the ideal itself has changed in nature. The experience to which literature exposes its writer and its reader has long been defined by Blanchot as a disruptive force. What has changed is Blanchot's relation to it. From having been *convergent* ("Classical works . . . appeared to come from somewhere above their time, tearing through it and burning it with an extreme intensity which concentrated within it the past, the present and the future"),[13] the domain of the literary has now become *divergent* ("The frenetic world . . . not only takes the place of the real world where we think we live our uneventful lives; in the process of destroying that world, it also destroys itself").[14] Increasingly, the silence of the writer is no longer simply a withholding of voice, or at best a retreat inward,[15] but the affirmation in writing of something absolutely destructive. It is an "irrational surplus" that lives on beyond the destruction of everything, including the individual subject through whom the affirmation is being made; a "nihilistic fury" akin to that of the warrior-hero who, to the outside world, takes on the appearance of a monumental statue, "but if we approach him, we realize that he is not there, and only a gap, an incomprehensible void indicate his existence." It is hardly surprising, though acutely relevant to our understanding of Blanchot's wartime writing, that in the face of the "nihilistic fury" of war Blanchot should ask: "compared to what it brings, is there any significance in the will to conquer and the hope of a people who resist?"[16]

It is important to bear in mind this fundamental change in Blanchot's relation to the literary ideal when we acknowledge that, while not physically in Clermont, he nonetheless finds himself, as a writer and a signature, in the company of some very different people from those with whom he spends his time in Paris. First there is the team of journalists who have kept the *Débats* going, many of whom were his close associates throughout the 1930s and who now appear to have capitulated to Vichy censorship and adopted its ideology. Then, more significantly, there are the authors whom Blanchot discusses. For it is here that the difficulties posed by his writing in this period come to a head. Crucially, writers such as Brasillach and Rebatet who used their weekly, *Je suis partout*, to promote pro-Nazi, anti-Semitic doctrines are never mentioned in Blanchot's articles.[17] Things become less straightforward, however, in the case of other known collaborators. Blanchot begins his reviewing in 1942 with articles on Montherlant[18] and Drieu la Rochelle, and indeed publishes a second article on Montherlant later in the year. In each case, it should be noted, this is ultimately in order to reject the very basis on which the thinking that inspires their attitude to the Occupation rests. In Drieu's case, Blanchot identifies a twofold failure at the heart of his worldview, and dismisses his efforts as "attempting the impossible."[19] As for Montherlant, despite his capacity for contesting everything, he appears as the unwitting prisoner of moral thinking of the most banal kind.[20]

However, whereas Drieu is examnied in a single study and with a dispatch that no doubt reflects a wish on Blanchot's part to be quite clear about where he stood during negotiations at the *NRF*, Montherlant, who was also a significant quantity in those negotiations,[21] is an author to whom Blanchot regularly returns throughout the occupation years.[22] And it is here that we come up against the true stumbling block for our reading of these chronicles. In his first essay on Montherlant in 1941, "The Writer and the Public," Blanchot presents him as a model of that literary detachment and rejection of circumstance that is required of any writer who is aware that his sole duty is to be loyal to himself. This sets a

pattern not only for Blanchot's recurrent interest in Montherlant, but for the very structure of his critical stance as the
national idyll falls apart: to take absolutely seriously and give
unqualified credence to any writer in whom the essential value
of writing is defended and acted upon, regardless of what
forms that writer's engagement with circumstance may take,
since the disappearance of France has drained circumstance of
all significance. Hence, Jacques Benoist-Méchin is twice made
the subject of one of Blanchot's chronicles, despite the fact
that he is the author of a sympathetic study of *Mein Kampf*,
as well as a vigorous advocate of full collaboration with Germany from within the Vichy government (he was condemned
to death in 1947 but the sentence was subsequently com-
muted).[23] On the literary side, three authors who attended the
Weimar Congress in 1941, Jacques Chardonne, Marcel Jouhandeau, and André Fraigneau, are given serious attention,
notwithstanding the complacency and compromise that affect
their respective positions at the time.[24] And epitomizing this
attitude, there is a throwaway reference to Charles Maurras,
whose study of ancient Greece, *Antinea*, is cited as all anyone
could ever need to read on the subject.[25]

We thus find ourselves obliged to acknowledge the following rather unpalatable fact: something at this time allows
Maurice Blanchot to ascribe value to the work of authors who
are generally seen in retrospect as having betrayed the basic
values of humanity though their behavior and their attitude
during the Occupation. And instinctively, the conclusion we
are tempted to draw from that is that Blanchot's own values
were compromised as a result. If literature considered as the
repository for the highest human values is defended by
Montherlant, a writer who, by contributing to a pro-Nazi
newspaper like *La Gerbe*, associated himself with collaborators
and anti-Semites, then there would seem to be something
wrong with literature understood thus, and wrong, therefore,
with its exponents and its defenders. This judgment lies at the
heart of what Blanchot has come to signify to his contemporaries, and while it simplifies matters for those who have

no time for him, for those who do, it remains something extremely difficult to confront, and a source of profound unease.

It is here that those who acknowledge Blanchot's value as a writer find themselves obliged to take a stand. The simplest and most generous option so far has been to acknowledge, as Blanchot himself did, that he was wrong, that what he wrote during the 1940s was fundamentally compromised, but that he changed, in a process that he himself called a *conversion*.[26] However generous this attitude may be, and however necessary it may appear as a counterweight to the extraordinary opprobrium that has become attached to Blanchot's name in influential circles, I would argue that it seriously restricts our understanding of Blanchot's work, by denying any significant relation between his thinking about literature up to the 1940s and the body of writing we now associate with his name.[27]

If, however, we approach Blanchot's writing not simply as the corpus of one individual, and see it, in its own historical development, as the site of a huge and fundamental change in Western values themselves (which is how successors like Foucault and Derrida approached it), we may, I believe, legitimately and productively adopt the following perspective: in the writing that Maurice Blanchot produced during the Occupation years, a new relationship is established, both critically and in practice, between literature and thought. Initially, Blanchot presents that relationship as something that continues to be bound up with what France signifies and is enshrined within a silence that marks a disdain for contemporary events. Very rapidly, however, this silent reserve ceases to provide a protected zone for the writer, and becomes the site of a falling away that affects everything: the world, the work, and the subject who seeks through language to bring them into relation. It is this transformation that is fundamental, in that it disrupts the basic convergence of the discourses of thought, literature and politics within a single value system, and the assumption that a unitary human ideal governs everything. An ideal of literary perfection that has always been essentially a source of division in Blanchot's thinking is deprived of the protective barrier of unified thought with the disappearance of France, and by 1942 it has turned the silent retreat of the writer into a site of endless divergence and effectively suspended individual subjectivity. It is this catastrophe that will turn the historical moment of France's defeat into a turning point for the very idea of history and the worldview it underpins. It is this *disaster* that Blanchot's writing will seek henceforth to contain and inscribe. Everything that we appreciate and learn from in Blanchot's writing right up to *The Writing of the Disaster* originates in the discontinuity out of which it arises.

In light of this, it is possible to view Blanchot's writing during the Occupation not as a regrettable hangover from a time when he was as it were not himself; nor, equally inadequately, as significant regardless of the limitations which compromise it, but rather as a key transitional phase in what we now know to be an exemplary project: the transformation of the Western subject and its worldview through writing. It is an undeniable fact that this phase is, of itself, imperfect, and readers today can only confirm what Blanchot holds out as a possibility: he was at best in the wrong, he was even at fault.[28] Because in his own mind the issue of collaboration and that of anti-Semitism had been clearly decided once and for all, it was of no interest to him whether a given writer subscribed to either or both, provided that in his writing, he recognized and responded to the disastrous ordeal onto which writing opened, and which for Blanchot constituted the sole reality henceforth. However, our consternation at this seeming absence of judgment is, I would argue, something that we, his readers can ultimately acknowledge and accept, in the knowledge that in 1942, the writer we expect better of is on the way to discovering an entirely new and original order of value.

There are sufficient guarantees of Blanchot's integrity during the Occupation years to make any aspersions cast upon it untenable. What is less well known is that the reputation as a Vichy newspaper that is usually attributed to the *Débats*, while undeniable in most respects, calls for a certain degree of qualification on closer examination of the individuals who contributed to it and the day-to-day content of the paper. A longstanding contributor, Guy Herpin, joined the Resistance in 1940. He was given instructions to infiltrate the Vichy establishment, and in 1942, he prevailed on the director of the *Débats*, Count Étienne de Nalèche, to let him return to the paper as its general secretary. He remained in this post until his arrest by the Gestapo in March 1944.[29] In January 1942 there appeared an article devoted to the Colorado beetle, which the French call *le doryphore*.[30] *Doryphore* was also a derogatory term for the German occupant at the time. While the article itself seems to make no play with the term, a response to it from a subscriber published a few days later entitled "A propos du doryphore" does.[31] Recalling that the *doryphore* is vulnerable to a parasite, the American uropod (*l'uropode d'Amérique*), its author wonders whether this has been forgotten since the previous invasion by the *doryphore*, and whether the remedy should not be tried a second time. In the light of America's entry into the war a month earlier, this letter would appear to be saying more than would initially appear.

A more substantial indication that all is not unanimous at the *Débats* can be found in October 1941 in a letter from "a long-time subscriber" (*un vieil abonné*) in response to Blanchot's first article on Paulhan's *Flowers of Tarbes*, "Terror in Literature."[32] The letter is entitled "In Defense of Clichés,"[33] and its author, who wishes to remain anonymous, indicates that the paper has already published a letter from him in response to another article of Blanchot's, "The Solitude of Péguy,"[34] entitled "Two Types of Solitude."[35] Unlike its author's previous contribution, "In Defense of Clichés" does not appear on the front page of the paper, which is given over to a celebration of the first anniversary of the meeting between

Hitler and Pétain in Montoire, which led to a politics of collaboration. After briefly going over what Blanchot says about
the problem of cliché for the writer, the author of the letter
shifts focus onto clichés of thought that, he says, are even
more harmful than clichés of language. "Banal ideas," it goes
on, "may well be hidden behind a brilliant, revolutionary
form. This would not be the first time that ideologies which
claim to be progressive [*d'avant-garde*] entered into a monstrous alliance with spiritually reactionary movements."

Once again, it is becoming clear that this correspondent
may have more to say than would first appear. On this anniversary day, the claim by the exponents of national revolution
to represent the future is being challenged. And this becomes
clearer as the letter goes on. Having shifted focus from language to thought, it now draws a distinction between the way
thoughts relate to their expression on one hand and to what it
calls "political and social contingencies" on the other. While
it would be too simple to say that the writer should be "of his
time," since "actuality will never be the same as the eternal,"
the only way to reach the eternal is to struggle constantly
against actuality. There is a fundamental difference between
simply being "of one's time" and living *in* one's time and
sometimes *against* it, and the struggle "is more or less easy,
depending on when one is alive." But in all cases, "courage of
thought consists basically of opposing collective or individual
betrayal, even when they are disguised behind a revolutionary
mask." In conclusion, the author of the letter insists on the
sterility of total withdrawal: "a language which tries to free
itself from life once and for all, even if it justifies this by some
mysterious inner logic, can only wither and die." And in an
unexpected turn, it cites the example of Bergson who, unlike
those who erroneously use his philosophy of intellectual purity
to justify a total retreat from the world, preferred "as he said
in his will to deprive himself of what would have been the
fulfillment of a natural tendency of his mind, rather than act
in a way that could have been interpreted as a betrayal of

loyalty." There can be no doubt that this is a reference to Bergson's decision in 1937 not to convert to Catholicism, so that he could remain alongside those who would very soon be the victims of persecution.[36] In the deafening silence within the columns of the *Débats* and elsewhere surrounding the relentless rise of anti-Jewish activity, the voice of this *vieil abonné* sounds a discreet yet decisive note.

Who could this correspondent be? It is not possible at present to know that. What is noteworthy is that it is Blanchot's writing that prompts the two responses; the ideas behind what he says about solitude and about rhetoric are both endorsed and made more radical by the *vieil abonné*; and by publishing these responses, the second one in particular, the *Débats* are opening their columns to arguments that are unmistakably seditious.

In 1942 another type of response, this time from within the paper itself, both complements those of the *vieil abonné* and helps to situate Blanchot more precisely. It comes in the form of signed articles by two regular contributors to the paper. One of them, Mario Meunier, made no secret of his commitment to Pétain and to a new Europe under the domination of Nazi Germany.[37] The other, Jean Mousset, had a very different outlook. The son of Albert Mousset[38] who was a long-standing contributor to the paper, he was a brilliant Slavicist who began writing occasionally for the *Débats* in the mid-1930s. In Yugoslavia at the outbreak of the war, he kept open the Institut Français in Belgrade until the German bombardment of April 1941, then returned to France. There, while becoming a regular contributor to the *Débats*, he quickly became involved with the Resistance, and eventually left for London and Algiers in the autumn of 1943.[39]

Meunier's article is a review of Dmitri Merezhkovski's *Dante*, a work that Blanchot had already reviewed in May.[40] Meunier agrees with Blanchot that the work adds nothing to what we know about Dante. However, he adds a rider to this. To the Italians, Dante has always represented the freedom of their nation: "what Dante seeks for his country and for himself is liberation and the supreme nobility of being free." However, a free nation requires the joy of being at peace, and "to deserve that peace, every people must subordinate its national life and its liberty to the life and liberty of universal order. To wish for the opposite . . . is to wish for fratricidal war to go on dividing the world. . . . To lose the world or to save it signifies, at this hour more than ever, a choice between the two: either eternal war . . . or eternal peace."

As a long-standing contributor to the paper, Meunier would certainly have been well aware of Blanchot's uncompromising nationalism and the resistance to Pétain's policy of collaboration which it continued to inspire, and his decision to return to Blanchot's essay on Dante and underscore the error of the nationalist position may be read in that context. However, what Jean Mousset writes is much more openly a challenge to Blanchot's position, though from the opposite angle. In an editorial on September 12–13, 1942, entitled "Portrait of a Hero" and devoted to the anniversary of the death of Guynemer, a World War I fighter ace, Mousset first observes that, a year after a previous editorial by him on the same subject, "never has the cult of the hero appeared more necessary."[41] And among those who have sometimes belatedly begun to define and praise what the hero stands for, he singles out Maurice Blanchot who in "a recent brilliant study" explored several definitions of the term.[42] Immediately, however, he expresses reservations about Blanchot's approach. "Perhaps," he writes, Blanchot "dwells too easily on the *unconscious* fury of the combatant." It would be much more accurate to say that what bursts forth in Guynemer is not blind rage, the frenetic *Wut* which Blanchot evokes, but the intense, burning awareness of a duty to be done, the idea that life would be unbearable without a certain ideal of honor or freedom. Repeating the terms of Blanchot's argument he goes on: "We keep hearing that heroism is 'organized madness' placed in the service of a religious or patriotic order." But "is this not to mistake the state of arousal into which war plunges the combatant for the goal of combat?" "Guynemer . . . was no Nietzschean hero," he goes on. "Guynemer's heroism is not that of the 'superman' who fights for the pure pleasure of fighting but that of a young man whose patriotic fervor transforms him into a demi-god." And he concludes with an invocation to Guynemer: "remind us constantly by the astounding example of your life that to be a hero is above all, in a world given over to materialism and violence, *to remain a man* and, if necessary, die for that cause."

If the letters from the *vieil abonné* indicate that Blanchot's thinking had its appeal for those who were opposed to Vichy's policies, the articles by Meunier and Mousset allow us, by a process of triangulation as it were, to see that for both camps, his position represented an unacceptable extreme: a nationalism too radical to allow collaboration, a notion of the hero which undermined the heroic self-sacrifice of the Resistance. And as we have seen, it is this position of extreme detachment from within the "irrational surplus" out of which it arises that most accurately reflects Blanchot's political and cultural choices in 1942. In a nice parallel, the position somewhere between resistance and collaboration into which Paulhan sought to insert Blanchot at the *NRF*,[43] is replicated at almost the same time, on the other side of the *ligne de démarcation*, by the responses of Mousset and Meunier. But whereas the *NRF* episode saw Blanchot effectively confined to a passive role, within the forum of the *Débats* that same in-between position, that of a "neither-nor" whose effect on the outside is an inactivity compounded by Blanchot's physical absence from where the paper is published, opens onto a dimension of subjectivity in writing where the collapse of impassioned nationalism into an ordeal of nothingness following the disappearance of France, becomes a search for a new form of subjectivity in writing. That is where Blanchot "is" in 1942: at the beginning of an exploration of what the discourse of literature can bring to the discourse of a subject who is effectively lost to the world. An exploration carried out not in alien, compromised territory, but in a forum whose overt collaborationism is rife with oppositional thinking.

In conclusion, it should be noted that Blanchot's writing in 1942 is not totally without its political edge. As Jeffrey Mehlman has argued, "The Politics of Sainte-Beuve," which exceptionally appeared on page one of the *Débats* in March 1942 (see this volume), contains a subtle yet powerful denunciation of the reasons behind collaboration with the occupant,[44] while on the same page, an article by another M. B., the regular editorialist Marcel Bastier, offers a eulogy of Pétain. But alongside Blanchot's article too there is a column by Pierre Bernus, who is also a regular contributor, bearing the title "A Fine Gesture" [Un beau témoignage]. This refers to a piece in the American journal *Collier's Weekly* entitled "Be Fair to France,"[45] which rejects the argument that the French defeat was a form of treachery and calls on Americans to celebrate France's instinctive love of freedom. Bearing in mind that the Americans had entered the war three months earlier, Bernus's piece appears in its turn to be a provocation, and after the American invasion of North Africa in November 1942, he would cease writing for the paper.[46] We do not know whether Blanchot himself placed his text on the front page or the editors of the paper made the decision to do so. Whichever is true, it seems clear that however detached from events and circumstance Blanchot's writing had become, the forum in which it appeared was no mere conformist backwater. Future research may show in greater detail what synergies were at work there, and whether the "desperate clarity" that was now inspiring his thinking allowed Blanchot to play a role in them.[47]

From the Middle Ages to Symbolism

The latest essay by Drieu la Rochelle, *Notes Toward an Understanding of the Century*,[1] provides a good example of the mirages that can cloud or distort a book in which general ideas appear. Nothing could be clearer than a work like this. In so far as we assume it to be systematic, we read it with ease and enjoy it as a coherent whole that we can understand, whose organization we can easily perceive and whose distinctly traced-out movement is one that we would not be so willing to follow, did we not also believe that we might occasionally be one step ahead of it. This is a pleasing impression, but one that is in fact deceptive and speciously designed to ensure our intellectual peace of mind. In fact, this book does not obey its own logic exclusively; it exists also in the gaps it contains, in what it withholds and in its constant rebellion against itself, which we initially interpret as the impulsiveness of its author's mind, and then as its most carefully composed and conscious mode of expression.

It is true that Drieu la Rochelle gives his reader fair warning, since his book appears with the title *Notes*, and these notes are presented as independent from and sometimes indifferent to each other. But the effect of such precaution is perhaps to deceive the reader rather than make him suspicious of his own satisfaction, since whereas the title and the project behind the work lead him to expect a fairly loose series of miscellaneous reflections, on reading them he is so struck by their coherence that he no longer sees anything but this unity, and readily summarizes the book's central ideas for himself, lazily believing that, thanks to this summary, he has grasped the entire book once and for all.

The problems that such a reading throws up are increased by the fact that to glean no more than one or two simple ideas from it does not make it unfaithful, or make us lose touch with its author once and for all. He himself does not appear to have wanted to conceal beneath his actual book a secret book that would differ totally from it and hold the key to what he truly thinks, and he is not averse to using a few simple words to sum up a complex explanation of history. On the contrary, that simplicity is something he accepts, but if he chooses it, it is out of a preference for decisiveness, promptness of mind and tempestuous impatience, and also because it is simplicity that reveals most consistently the complex demands of thought, its defiance of the abyss, the challenges in the course of which it both puts itself to death and comes to its own rescue.

Notes Toward an Understanding of the Century contains a paean to the Middle Ages, a critique of rationalism and a sympathetic analysis of the most recent political and literary movements of the twentieth century. The Middle Ages marked a privileged moment of Christian civilization, when a perfect equilibrium between body and soul found expression during a period of youth rather than already weary maturity, and with all the vigor of a strong and carefree state of mind. The Middle Ages represent a period in which things blossomed before giving way, behind a mask of perfection and with an alibi provided by the most brilliant and prosperous eras, to a period of almost constant decline and an often invisible but always identical effort aimed at breaking with a harmony whose secrets have since been lost. From the eighteenth century onward, rationalism separates and divides man, threatens reason by transforming it into a mediating power entirely turned in on itself, destroys the body by humiliating it through the triumph of the machine, and provokes a vain, confused reaction that, under the name of Romanticism, destroys all hope of salvation through the superficial way it makes use of it. The decline continues, therefore, necessarily becoming deeper and requiring of those who have the task of taking it forward a dizzying sense of failure, a vainglorious craving for the abyss and an admirable capacity for obedience to nothingness, all of which are powers that tend toward awakening the soul from its death. It is thus that Symbolism comes into being, and along with Symbolism, various intellectual movements that, from Rimbaud to Paul Claudel, signify the rebirth of a genuine spirituality. At the same time, through sport and a taste for physical adventure, the body acquires a new dignity; it is now fit to play a role in the historical upheavals that mark the end of rationalism. The restoration of the body and the awakening of the soul offer the twentieth century, in the powerful political movements that unite them, the opportunity for a blossoming that is comparable to that of the Middle Ages.

It goes without saying that, like all thinking that is applied to history and reconstructs its development by means of one or two very general statements, Drieu la Rochelle's remarks will probably provoke endless objections and some stout opposition. His celebration of the Middle Ages can be accused of being both arbitrary and unoriginal. The idea of a progressive decline that, from the thirteenth century onward, drives history toward a desperate outcome that it escapes, after seven centuries of exhaustion, through an almost instantaneous triumph, may well appear preposterous. It may appear incomprehensible that, having offered a justifiable critique of the myth of progress, he should restore it in reverse, either by endowing history with an inexorable dialectic of decadence, or more subtly by creating, between points in time that are irrevocably separate, audacious linking roads, passes that demolish mountains, abysses, and precipices, in short, everything that makes genuine historical mountaineering impossible. That much can be said, and naturally a lot more besides. But to take issue in this way seems superfluous, since it presupposes the same abstract impatience we think we are right to complain about, and it ignores some of the intentions that can clarify the work most effectively. In fact, whether the medieval era in which Drieu la Rochelle sees a model of civilization corresponds to the image that observers today can form of it is no more than a private matter between professional academics and amateur historians. What is truly interesting is to perceive the ideal to which, through the medium of a historical myth, a writer in search of his own movement finds himself attracted.

It quickly becomes clear that these *Notes* do not contain a simple apology for the soul and the body, but rather present equilibrium as an ambivalent form of struggle, an energetic and furious display of forces that achieve a balance within a state of limitless tension. In the Middle Ages there was certainly no equilibrium, but rather a state of division whose effect was to separate all forms of life into very distinct classes and categories: the clergy, the laity, the monastic life, the chivalric condition. This division had as its symbol the two sacraments that make up holy communion: bread for the laity, wine for the clergy. Inspired by this power with two faces, it was in society itself that a synthesis occurred, and not in people's hearts, and that synthesis could all the more readily be a reconciliation of violently distinct elements, because the clash of these opposing terms did not jeopardize an individual's destiny, and found expression in powerfully hierarchical structures. Drieu la Rochelle has retained from this view of the Middle Ages the idea of an equilibrium that is at no point a state of repose, a harmony that appears when contradiction is taken to its extreme. Soul and body form a union that is cease-lessly struggling against itself, that contests and consolidates itself by rejecting all conciliation and finally comes face to face with itself in a paroxysm of contrasts. What he is in search of is excess considered as equilibrium, something uncontainable and impossible considered as an ultimate accord, and this superior motive power, this effort at overcoming which some-times appears in the soul, sometimes in the body, represents an aspiration whose culmination, in a well-ordered civiliza-tion, is expressed not in tumult and catastrophic upheaval, but in a state of perfect regularity, a proud combination of restraint and delirium, of night and day.

It is understandable that Drieu la Rochelle should have dis-covered in Symbolism those demands that appear to him to be essential and should wish to show that true, deep Romanticism began in our country only when Gérard de Nerval, Mallarmé, Rimbaud, and Lautréamont, drowning with their silence the vain cries of poets whose revolt was a mere sham, raised ques-tions of extreme complexity that placed them directly in con-tact with the absolute. But if the important pages in which he recognizes that French Symbolists tapped into an authentic spirituality anticipate the conclusion of his book, it can be said that they also make that conclusion problematical, by assum-ing a straightforward collaboration between Symbolism con-sidered as a restoration of the soul, and modern political forces considered as a restoration of the body. Alongside all of its weakness and incoherence, the principle characteristic of Sym-bolism, or rather of the spiritual concerns which it translates, is that it expresses a total demand, lays claim to every possibil-ity and tolerates nothing but the world it rends asunder and the lightning bolt with which it does so. If there is one conces-sion it cannot accept, it is to be given no more than its due. It proudly flaunts its own impossibility as what justifies it essen-tially, and it insolently rejects every piece of verbal trickery that seeks, on the grounds that it aspires to totality, to include it alongside other no less totally demanding notions within a har-mony of opposing wills.

In a certain sense, if one adopts the perspective that Drieu la Rochelle sets up, it is clear that Symbolism and "political athletics," to the extent that each of them seeks to take all human reality to the extreme limit of what is possible, can come together only in an insurmountable contradiction, a final clash from which nothing could be salvaged. They have in common not the fact that they are complementary, but that they reject all complementarity out of hand; and indeed they only provide man with anything at all because they both claim to provide him with everything. The tragic, and in certain respects comic, side of this situation is that these two movements, which are meaningful only if they are complete and which would consequently cease to be anything whatsoever if they allowed themselves to become complete, are both equally incapable of representing a true concern for humanity with all of its demands. The one, which is a grafting of literature onto an exhausted spirituality, ultimately fails, in the full knowledge that literature can never entirely carry within it the destiny of man; the other, unaware of its defeat, believes it is succeeding because, by being called on to act immediately, it becomes absorbed in day-to-day developments that are basically nothing but pure diversion. The advantage of the former is that it sees the impasse to which it is doomed, and leaves behind superficial yet sparkling images of it. The merit of the latter is that it provides, in its thirst for physical furor, the material equivalent of a true adventure, which is the deepest need of a human being. It is obviously tempting, in response to this twofold failure, to imagine an alliance that would coordinate these two projects and mutually reinforce them. This is the alliance for which Drieu la Rochelle has imagined the conditions, and that he has studied the way one studies a dream, with resolute serenity, calm logic, a burning desire for equilibrium, and all the optimistic qualities that are particularly necessary in writers who know they are attempting the impossible.

—January 15, 1942

A Novel by Colette

The novel that Colette has just published, *Julie de Carneilhan*,[1] brings to mind a book whose author would seem to have had only one purpose: to scale the novelist's art down to its functional elements alone. It is in a way an act of soul-searching, and any true writer will feel the need to submit to this ordeal at least once in his life. Rather than write a work that sums him up, rather than express the complexity of his talents, his richly creative powers and all of the resources he has within him and of which he is only partly aware, his intention is to bring forth a work for which he is entirely responsible, and in relation to which he can only be either guilty or suspect, never innocent. His intention is also to seek out everything that is superfluous in his art: the beauties that enhance it but that can be sacrificed to it without it suffering as a consequence, the forms that are not smooth but diversely broken up, and that adorn it with infinitely reflected light, in a word everything that makes it visible and allows it to appear external to itself. It is these outer charms that he erases; he struggles against tendencies that seemed essential to him until then; he takes a

severe scalpel to those organs he can do without, mutilating
himself not only like those classical statues that are only complete when they are lacking an arm, but getting dangerously
close to the heart, which he aims for while stopping short of
doing it actual harm. In fact, he seeks to perform an act of
literary analysis on himself *in vivo*, and by creating a work that
has been stripped totally bare, is without accidents and reduced to only those elements without which it would not
exist, he renders quite impossible the work of the commentator, who can only ever reconstruct artistic endeavor indirectly,
by means of its accidents and its incidental riches.

Given its subject, Colette's novel is not designed to deceive
its reader about the world she requires in order to give expression to her fiction. There is nothing unexpected about the
story she has chosen. The handful of incidents which make up
the life of Julie de Carneilhan appear to us like a series of
images borrowed from her other works. The story of this age-
ing woman who has twice been married and now has an insignificant lover and an idiotic friend; a woman with no worries
and no passion and who lives from one hour to the next with
no thought for anything except what the moment requires of
her, is the same story as that of numerous shadowy figures on
whom Colette has already based her best novels. What is
more, her intention in her latest book is to bring this story
fully to the fore, since by itself it makes up the entire novel,
while allowing us no illusions as to its scope. The plot is everything and also nothing at all. It is merely an account of some
insignificant facts, and these facts are revealed in all their insig-
nificance. Furthermore, Colette avoids the trap of that naturalism of bygone days that sought to outdo the mediocrity of
existence, and filled large books with very little so that it could
be said: such is life. Colette does not betray the world she
writes about. It is not possible, once we have read her book,
to dismiss the little dramas of her heroine as vain commotion. If Julie de Carneilhan still has a fleeting preference for
her second husband, who left her; if she attempts to coax a

reciprocal gesture from him and if in the end she is taken in by her hopes, these barely sketched-out impulses are simultaneously shades of nothing and the essence of a solemn tragedy. No one dwells on their significance; the heroine herself shuns any thought which might prove an impediment, and she is incapable of rising to a real drama; but the tragic elements are nevertheless there, and the fact that they are scattered throughout an aimless life, the fact that the flame of despair and the horror of impotent love only fleetingly traverse a fragile heart, and seen from without have no more importance than any other momentary sensation, in short this reduction of tragedy to one sensation among others gives the work its secret heart and prolongs it beyond what it is.

It is easy to see everything that Colette has ejected from her novel. There are none of those observations whose only reason for being there is their liveliness and spontaneity. Gone are the impressions that swirl eagerly around an image. Amorous dalliance is either excised or suppressed. The mysterious charm that comes from the exquisite company of an animal has no place in this book, where art retains only what it cannot do without and still survive. Nature is barely visible. There is the occasional memory of a distant country manor, an allusion to seasons blurring into each other, to mist over fresh water as day begins, to country paths lined with gorse, unripe mulberries and spiny burdock. But such reminiscence is quickly dispelled, leaving merely an arid world, empty of faces and understanding looks, in which a sparse and empty plot provides no external interest, a world dominated exclusively by the sundry impressions that fill a person's life.

There is no work of Colette's in which sensations play a greater role, yet find themselves more comprehensively reduced to their bare essentials. In certain respects, the entire book is merely the story of the sensations that absorb the attention of each and every person every day. "It must be Friday, thought Mme de Carneilhan who had scarcely woken up. I can smell fish." Such remarks as these make up the fabric of time; they are merely fleeting images, feelings mingled with rapid perceptions, actions whose only trace is their external outline. Mme de Carneilhan turns off the gas, leaves the "china" casserole on the stove, lays out the "Empire" cup, the "Swedish" spoon, a loaf of "rye" bread; "the smell" of the "hot" chocolate makes her yawn. She is led along unthinkingly by her actions as they adhere to objects whose contact alone, through the sensation it awakens, constitutes reality. Mme de Carneilhan is vaguely aware that she is touching a cup, and she registers through an act of semiconscious recognition the halo of sensation that accompanies her act. Her most practical actions are enhanced by a delicate purity of touch. Her entire life is divided between spontaneous acts and a few sensory relations with things, momentary sparks whose light goes out as soon as it is glimpsed.

It might be thought that this way of privileging the external impressions upon which people depend during their lives, and which form the detached, spiritual dimension of their existence, would tend to create a shimmering, iridescent work in which gleams, smells, sounds and all the myths of the body abound in a skillfully contrived confusion. But this is where the art of Colette appears in its true light. Not only does it seek to elude the resources which the facile allure of sensuality can provide; not only does it reduce sensuality to the sensuousness of eyes, nostrils or ears, but it keeps sensations strictly under control, and far from being engulfed by a whirlwind of impressions, or throwing itself into chaotic to-ing and fro-ing, swirls of fleeting images or imperceptible nuances, it imposes strict, rare, and stylized contours on sensation. Nothing is more clear-cut than this world whose entire reality lies in the inconsistency of what is tangible. Precise epithets cause objects to burst their outer shell, and beneath the colors that illuminate them, preserve the structure without which they would vanish. The sensations that predominate are those that are best suited to expressing material reality and perceptible form. Even the nuances that enclose forms in a mesh of indistinction are free of shadow. They are seen in a harsh light. Haloes, fog and drowsiness are all made distinctly visible.

It is through a singular combination of sensory intensity and stylization, of order and pure impression, through a concern for rigor within vagueness and restraint within physical obsession that Colette's art has reached a pitch of perfection. In her personal universe, where what appears is the warmth of a fur or a hand, and where everything desperately abandons itself to the most fleeting sort of life, what finally prevails is a feeling of abstract dignity, as if appearances could only be revealed through the most calculated choices, inflexible in their precision and rigor. Her style constantly combines the qualities that allow her to grasp the most tangible aspects of the world using the least physical aspects of language. It is wary of images, and its syntax will only allow precise and solid linkages, without those fluid slippages that numb the attention and distract the mind. Adjectives with their own inherent expressive value, which do not mutually cancel each other out through their sensuous contradictions and which, in a perfect gesture of approval, provide the most isolated noun with the physical form it requires; verbs that always stand alongside an action and describe it themselves in all its nuances; and finally a modest panoply of faintly ludicrous expressions, crude detail, and piquant terms (this is the price to be paid when style does without images but cannot do without the picturesque), all these features compose a system of expression in which everything is movement, firmness of line, speed of decision, and that brings to light what is most obscure and indeterminate in the realm of the senses.

It is therefore totally wrong to define this art as a form of impressionism. As well as not meaning much at all, that word implies that the world of the novel is plunged into a play of light and shadow, enclosed within a semitransparent envelope in which forms, figures and events are lost among the myriad nuances into which they are refracted. In this respect, if Colette's work is compared to the admirable works of Virginia Woolf, *Mrs Dalloway* in particular, it becomes clear to what extent a book like *Julie de Carneilhan* excludes furtive images, intelligible blurrings or visions that gleam then scatter within an uninterrupted duration. *Mrs Dalloway* tells of a day in the life of Clarissa Dalloway, and of a day in London at the same time. Virginia Woolf described her own intentions in these lines, which may stand as a definition of all art that is devoted to time: "Examine for a moment an ordinary mind on an ordinary day. The mind receives myriad impressions—trivial, fantastic, evanescent, or engraved with the sharpness of steel. From all sides they come, an incessant shower of innumerable atoms; and as they fall, as they shape themselves into the life of Monday or Tuesday, the accent falls differently from of old; the moment of importance came not here but there. . . . Is it not the task of the novelist to convey this varying, this unknown and uncircumscribed spirit, whatever aberration or complexity it may display, with as little mixture of the alien and external as possible? We are not pleading merely for courage and sincerity; we are suggesting that the proper stuff of fiction is a little other than custom would have us believe."[2] This is a remarkable project. In fact, however, the English novelist was the victim of a misunderstanding. Her purpose, so it seemed to her, was to express life with more sincerity and more simplicity ("Life," she wrote, "is not a series of gig lamps systematically arranged"),[3] whereas in fact she was destined, through a choice which was itself quite arbitrary and as it were a type of myth, to capture the pure and evanescent movement of time. If her aesthetic could be compared to that of the Impressionist painters, it was to the extent that she could say like Monet: there is no such thing as "the" haystack, "the" cathedral, "the" poplar; there is the haystack and there is the cathedral, at a given hour and in a given light, that is to say the unbroken course of time.

Nothing could be further removed from this myth of pure duration than the work of Colette. The French novelist is willing to follow time only by way of the events that translate it, just as she only grasps sensations through a reality that does not fade away. There is in her books a commitment to naturalness that rejects excess, is disdainful of artistic license and is based on a choice. The mysterious impression left by her most translucent pages comes from this sobriety, this silence through which we must pass in order to follow the movements of her characters and her stories. Everything here is simple, everything proceeds quickly and discreetly to its end. And all that remains at the close is a memory of obstinate stylization, of skillful resistance to words, and of the almost mechanical ease with which she uses ellipsis and foreshortening. All of this, combined with an impassioned attempt to convey physical effect, produces an art that is more conscious and deliberate than it is instinctive.

—February 3, 1942

Bergson and Symbolism

It has been observed that for some months now, poetry seems to have appealed to more minds than was the case before the war, and this observation has led to conclusions that have generally been a source of comfort.[1] Such remarks can hardly be taken seriously. If there really are a lot of young poets, let us hope that their silence will not be disturbed, that they will not feel dependent upon public taste, that their anguish and their personal struggle will have a greater goal than that of simply being read, published and applauded by overzealous sympathizers. On more than one occasion we have read that poetry offers a refuge for both writers and readers by making a disinterested culture accessible to them in difficult times. It would naturally be ridiculous, in response to such vulgar observations, to recall what a perilous exercise poetry constitutes for a very few. To say that poetry is a refuge is to say that, by turning in on oneself towards the inner source of all tragedy and seeking to communicate it at any cost is, by comparison with external circumstances, to experience a moment of respite and to yield to despair as if it were a state of repose.

Does that make any sense? Suffice it to say, once and for all, that it is better to talk as little as possible about poetry, or else only to talk about it when form and technique are the issue.

It is what makes it a straightforward, vigorous piece of work on a subject that generally leads to confusion that prompts us to cite the recent book by Emeric Fiser on symbol and symbolism, *The Literary Symbol*.[2] In it, pages full of precise, well-organized argument overseen by solid scholarly method are devoted to Symbolist art from Wagner to Marcel Proust, and seek to clarify the meaning of the word symbol in those works that can be linked to the so-called Symbolist school. Fiser studies symbol in so far as symbol was used to refer to a literary doctrine. He does not consider it as an ideal faculty of the mind, a higher instrument of expression whose effects could be observed in all literature and all poetry, whatever the period. He touches more on literary history than on criticism, which is concerned with techniques of the mind, and he is ready to offer a limited conclusion, if that conclusion results in replacing so-called general ideas and vague aesthetic tendencies with clear and practical definitions.

The main interest of the book lies in a study of Symbolism as Bergson's philosophy allows us to understand it. It is well known that through his critique of language, his wish to explore the life of the deeper self outside of intellectual and social convention, and his philosophy of intuition and *durée*, Bergson provided art with a theoretical heritage that was more a justification for the works of the great Symbolists than their source As we know, language for Bergson is an instrument forged by intelligence and action for expressing concepts, states, and indeed everything that has space as either its fabric or its image. But in return, it allows the mobility of consciousness, the dream of inner life and everything that has its source and its reality in *durée* to disappear. The mind cannot communicate itself directly. It is only indirectly, through a difficult invocation and by turning language back on itself, that it can bring about an authentic revelation, while exorcising the banality of words, their exchange value and their social significance. The transfiguration of language in response to the demand of living memory is what Symbolism takes as its goal, and the means it has given itself count for little compared to the wealth of thinking that such an ambition presupposes.

Fiser abandons the heights of these general considerations to analyze the various elements contained within the literary symbol. He distinguishes four of them. Symbol exists if words or images, thanks to new permutations, are rescued from the meaning which made them crystallize into commonplaces; if words and images, thus renewed, appear through the play of analogies as if they were linked to the deeper life they are meant to reflect; if this way of exposing an analogy gives rise to an emotion that reflects its power to enchant; and finally, the beauty and the value of a symbol depend on the memories that are bound up with it, since the fundamental innocence that must be attained is indistinguishable from the flow of *durée* and from the past. Fiser accompanies his argument with examples taken from Baudelaire, Mallarmé, and, above all, Marcel Proust. It is clear that symbol appears to him as a moving composition that is very difficult to grasp in its parts, and that cannot become a subject for analysis, since it becomes something other as soon as it is immobilized and broken down into its elements. The literary symbol is neither a pure word, nor an image momentarily shackled to another, nor a veiled idea which those images might explore; it is not a presence but a potential for movement, a direction for thought, an intention that cannot be grasped at any point, and whose passage is perceptible, behind the words and forms of language, as the shadow of a radiant dispersal and the hope that a seed will germinate.

These considerations have become familiar in our era, and in his study of myth, Jacques Rolland de Renéville has shown in what ways similes, metaphors, and symbols provide the keys to a veritable doctrine of analogy, capable of opening up a perspective on the deepest levels of existence.[3] The enduring lesson of Fiser's work would seem to be that there are perhaps disadvantages in looking for a basis for symbolism or even a metaphysical law of symbol in Bergson's philosophy. It goes without saying that Bergson's research coincided roughly speaking with the creative initiatives of the end of the nineteenth century, and that they can be seen as a remarkably apposite justification of the latter. But if it is natural not to lose sight of the correspondences between symbolist poetry and the philosophy of intuition, it is equally the case that we run the risk of falsifying the creative act of the poet by applying to it the framework of a theoretical explanation and the forms taken by enigmas that have already been solved. Method makes very little sense in the case of literary problems in general, and it makes no sense at all as far as poetic problems are concerned. It is the poets themselves who must guide us, through their works and sometimes through the awareness they had of the means they employ, toward that crucial point on which the diverse powers of their creations converge, like paths that are both identical and separate.

—February 10, 1942

Tales and Stories

Authors no longer publish books of short fiction, people are sometimes heard to complain, because they think the public prefers a long novel to a selection of shorter stories. Perhaps that is true. A few years ago, Paul Morand agreed to edit a new collection with the optimistic title *Rebirth of the Short Story*. But the short story did not enjoy a revival. People went on reading numerous pleasant and insignificant tales in periodicals that saw the need for them. Other more worthwhile ones could also be read, inspired by German Romanticism or obeying the edicts of French Surrealism. These were sometimes very fine works, and there would be a case for seeking them out and collecting them together one day. And Marcel Aymé wrote charming narratives that effortlessly made people like them. That is all, and perhaps it is a great deal.

Theorists have always liked to distinguish between the short story and the novel, and to imagine the different laws that these separate stars are said to obey. Jean Giraudoux, who seemed content after a first book of stories to make short stories out of the splendid leftovers from his novels, wrote some very instructive pages about the genre, but omitted to include them in his recent volume of criticism.[1] But the problem will constantly find new devotees and new solutions, with little likelihood that such research will ever give rise to any decisive observations. We find ourselves in a period when the novel as a literary work, obeying nothing but its own disorder or more accurately, its prose, which appears an enigma, has only the loosest of connections with the existence of art in general. It is thus perhaps rather futile to look for definitions and rules in the case of species about whose genus we have almost no knowledge.

Two books that have just appeared do not correspond exactly to the usual conventions governing volumes of short stories, and each of them is made up of separate narratives. One of them has proved highly pleasurable to read. Continuing the series of the *Astonishments of Guillaume Francoeur*, which is devoted to the whims of a lazy, carefree humanism, André Fraigneau has brought together under the title *The Prime of Life* several traveler's tales and one or two lighthearted adventures whose form is utterly charming.[2] In Perpignan and in Port-Vendres, in the Greece of Olympia and in a Venice rejuvenated and refreshed by the outlook of youth, then finally during the days during 1940 when France was enduring the exodus, Guillaume Francoeur observes the world and, through the grace of his youth, good taste, and joy, provides images of it that seem plucked from some dazzling springtime. André Fraigneau's style has acquired an alluring freedom, poised delightfully at a point of perfect balance between the artificial and the natural. His first works were composed in a flutter of countless wings amid the tentative grace of their images and metaphors. Between words and things they forged secret friendships, ironic complicities, a whole secret and graceful state of errancy, but such diversions still remained haphazard and only played a part in the story itself by providing a dash of elegance. In *The Prime of Life* the shadows and schemes of the words give rise to a perfectly natural and well-organized narrative; we are as close as possible to a simple account of things we can see and hear. Perpignan is Perpignan; the gods of Olympia are those who come to life before the eyes of all those travelers who delight in them. And yet this world, which is entirely without falsification and eternally present in what fleetingly passes, finds expression in a form that dances, leaps, and offers gifts, perfumes, and colors amidst a gentle tumult of preciosity.

It must be admitted that Guillaume Francoeur's adventures amount to very little: a meeting in Port-Vendres with a girl who only goes out at night; a meeting in Loutraki with a young woman who is offered then snatched from him in the course of some dubious affair; a meeting in Venice with a child whose mystery is its innocence: these are slender melodies, played and preserved by an obliging flute. However, this meager substance, these idle, airy nothings are more than just a pretext for descriptions designed purely to be memorable. The shadow of an adventure that is briefly visible therein depends so perfectly on the place where it happens, matches so faithfully the world from which it comes that the roses, the trellis-work and the stars that it brings into being light up the landscape, the town and the fine gardens it is designed to illustrate, in a fleeting revelation. They are phantoms that fade, like fleeting signs of more durable encounters. The shadows here precede the fine stonework, the masterpieces of light and incense that we encounter at famous sites, and that the studied admiration of the traveler offers to the memory of those who have never seen anything for themselves.

Another of the charms of these stories comes from the fact that if they draw life from mere trifles, they are nevertheless the site of endlessly beguiling episodes. The least detail of a voyage becomes in the eyes of the astonished Francoeur a sequence of mysteries, an opportunity for pathetic curiosity, the first thread in a web whose extraordinary figures cannot be predicted and that, even if it tears on a mere illusion, gives pleasure through its transparency and its movement. During a dreamy walk through Olympia that is part inspired and part mocking, the young traveler glimpses the naked body of a young man hidden among the reeds. "It's unbelievable," he says. "I have just come across Daphnis!" And this image gives rise to a fascinating story in which insignificant incidents become a figure for mysterious destinies and nurture interminable reveries. Is this Daphnis who bears the mark of misfortune a young madman? Is he born of the sun whose dark burn he bears? Did he eventually kill himself in order to awaken for one last time, with a violent rifle shot, the peaceful echoes of the valley at the gates of Arcadia? No matter: from this fragile silken thread the author spins the pleasure of infinite hours.

But as there is in everything, however insubstantial, the haze of a sort of philosophy, along with these images André Fraigneau occasionally offers for our amusement the trap of an ulterior motive. Guillaume Francoeur is witness to the privileged moments of passing time; he is the happy, roving hero for whom, without special machinery or ingenious invention, the grace of time and the world becomes accessible. In the harmony of certain sky-tones and certain monuments, certain faces and certain paintings, in the refinement of certain gestures, as in the beauty of a smile or an adventure, there is a joyous and delightful miracle whose encounter makes lying unnecessary. André Fraigneau gave one of his earlier works the title *Human Grace*.[3] In *The Prime of Life* he once again displays that grace that comes close to catastrophe, mingles with ugliness and indifference, breaks apart beneath too insistent a gaze and with the light of a fine day creates effigies in marble or bronze, anonymous portraits, in short, all that is robust and durable in a civilization doomed to decadence.

The five Guillaume Francoeur stories (the last of which, "The Countryside of France," seems spoiled by needless political allusions and a degree of complacent childishness) draw their unity from their preoccupation with those hours of delight that, in periods of refined culture, achieve eternity in perfect works, be they a sculpture or a temple. There is also a highly visible unity to the volume of tales Robert Francis has just published with the title *Stories from Scripture*.[4] In fact, Robert Francis has been too modest to do full justice to the beauty and depth of the project he has been tempted by. Feeling drawn to certain episodes from the Bible, he has sought to rewrite them by adapting them to the familiar framework of contemporary life. To make use of themes from Scripture is a project that has appealed to many a writer before him. Anatole France expended painstaking erudition on the task. Jules Lemaître made it the object of charming but soon forgotten fantasies. Closer to us, and with greater success, Thomas Mann has drawn from the Bible one of the most important and significant works of contemporary literature. We would not wish to compare the *Story of Joseph* trilogy with a book of tales displaying infinitely less ambition. By descending into the well of the past and seizing hold of some wondrous figures, what Thomas Mann envisaged was a profound evocation of the myth of time, and a search for a symbolic creation. In the minds of all those who have read *The Story of Jacob*,[5] the account of the death of Isaac will remain as an image of a supreme art. On the point of leaving this world, Isaac who prophesies and speaks of himself as a victim spared by heaven, Isaac who foretells Christ's sacrifice suddenly begins to bleat, and believing he has turned into the animal previously sacrificed in his place, he comes really to resemble the ram. The significance of this episode is extraordinary. That primordial bleating, which is an allusion to the paschal lamb and a reminder of the prehistoric beast that the clan takes as its idol, echoes down through history. It is the expression of what remains fearful in the most authentic holiness, and of what is holy before all holiness. It is the echo of the origin and the voice of what soon will be accomplished. It draws time wondrously in on itself.

Robert Francis's *Stories from Scripture* are utterly remote from these mythic notions. All they are left with are stories in which patriarchs relive their lives in our midst, among the encumbrances of modern existence. Cain and Abel become music-hall acrobats; Noah is a humble Paris tradesman; Joseph still reads fortunes in the stars, but Potiphar's wife is a precise and determined businesswoman. Job is a rich merchant and runs the Early Morning Waste and Natural Fertilizer Company, whose advertising slogan is "Big Job's for Manure." Robert Francis clearly finds amusement in what anachronism has to offer. On the way, there are one or two pleasures and one or two surprises to be had, but generally the result is one of boredom, except where an ingenuity that is entirely taken up with the simple things of life gives some worth to what is imprisoned inside all this futile fakery.

It must be admitted that some of the tales collected in *Stories from Scripture* appeal to the authority of the Bible to very little avail, and retain from its great dreams no more than a name that no longer corresponds to anything. Job is the story of a rich man who has never known a day's rest, whose weariness is proving the ruin of him and who is happy with a poverty that will allow him a new departure. Samson is by nature a strong man brought low by women, and who will be true to himself only through committing a crime. Joseph, encouraged by Potiphar's wife, becomes a famous astrologer whose advertising signs are fixed to the Eiffel Tower. These are pointless fantasies, more like puns, and one wonders in all innocence how such radiant, terrible names could end up lost in stories that offer merely vague reminiscences. But other tales lead back more skillfully to their source. In them, a gentle ingenuity surrounds the images that deck themselves out unpretentiously in modern colors. You yield to the ambiguous sense of freshness and playfulness that these images bring with them. And you accept them as shades that have followed history in its sluggish drift, and which in the present no longer consist of anything except absence and infidelity.

—March 3, 1942

The Politics of Sainte-Beuve

After an important volume on the subject of *Sainte-Beuve's Thought*, Maxime Leroy has now devoted a new book to *Sainte-Beuve's Politics* that displays great subtlety and learning.[1] Maxime Leroy connects with his subject through such assiduous interaction, in a process of such perfect intellectual and moral exchange, that he appears to have decided to study Sainte-Beuve by coming to resemble him totally. Referring to an article of his on Ballanche, whose sympathetic tone had shocked his friends, Sainte-Beuve wrote that he had "so to speak changed into him to such a degree that he had been taken for his double." Similarly, it is no mere tranquil curiosity about Sainte-Beuve that inspires Maxime Leroy. What draws him to the writer is admiration placed in a state of constant alarm. He wants to admire and understand in all circumstances; he wants to go as deep as possible and for these depths never to be mediocre. All the difficult moments in the writer's life, those which have allowed commentators who dislike him to see him as an envious spirit, prone to change his views, more concerned with peace of mind than with conviction and cruelly devoid of generosity, elicit the highest levels of attention, fidelity and vigilance from Maxime Leroy. He struggles forcefully to dispel every shadow. He permits himself no reservations. He finds the best in the worst. And thanks to his extraordinary understanding of hidden circumstances, this partisan prejudice rarely gives the impression that it is clouding clear-sighted vision.

This book contains various observations concerning the attitude that writers adopt when confronted with historical upheavals. Sainte-Beuve witnessed the 1830 revolution, the revolution of 1848, and the coup d'état of December 2. He was involved in them as an observer and not as a partisan. Freer than Chateaubriand, Lamartine, or Victor Hugo, and also more able to apply his mind where others were in the grip of passion, he nevertheless refused to remain on the sideline, and his own abundant curiosity, combined with an enduring concern for social realities, led him to express in a wide variety of ways the movements of a mind buffeted by short-lived storms. Maxime Leroy writes that Sainte-Beuve's mind is far from being purely or even especially literary; his stock lies elsewhere in his view: in the area of social and political concerns. And while explaining what is sometimes disappointing about his criticism of literary works, this diversity of attention, this rare and precious alignment with the circumstances which are those of a given society, endows what he says about men and his times with a power that displays both wisdom and novelty.

The 1830 revolution surprised Sainte-Beuve as much as it surprised the king, his ministers, and the conspirators. Those who had wished for it experienced the same violent discomfiture as those who feared it. The innovators were taken by surprise, said Sainte-Beuve, and Armand Carrell makes a similar admission: "We were there, we all saw it, all of us who speak of it and discuss it today, but let us be honest, we understood nothing about it." Eighteen years later there is the same surprise, the same dismay, mingled with a tragic sense of absurdity. "What extraordinary events!" says Sainte-Beuve. "What a dream! I was expecting many things, but not so immediately, and not of this type." And a few weeks later, Lamartine writes something that Barbès, Karl Marx, Tocqueville, or Hugo could have written: "The February revolution surprised me as much as it did everyone else." In both cases, political violence put an end to a regime that Sainte-Beuve disliked: a number of his friends and also his preferences are caught up in the riots: even in 1848, "a fatal year of folly," he confides to his secretary Troubat that "his sympathies were generally with the insurgents." But in both cases, too, he feels a harsh disdain for those on whom the revolution has bestowed a new legality, seeing them as victors who are terrified of their own victory, either incapable of mastering it or greedily intent on turning it to their own advantage. In July 1833, he says to Adam Mickiewicz: "You say you are pilgrims and in exile, and we too have been exiled from the revolution we loved and brought about; we have been expelled from our hopes."

This surprise, crowned by disappointment and perhaps a sort of fright, reflects a profound judgment on the men he has seen pitted against each other in these great circumstances. A fact he discovers very quickly is that reason is lacking in both those who govern and those who are governed; both sides are blind, irresponsible, and foolhardy; they yield to the folly of systems or the weight of tradition; their actions take place in either a debauch of reason or a turmoil of instincts. Weary like Guizot or hotheaded like Barbès, they perish from either anarchy or an excess of coherence. "French society in 1830," he writes, "was in such a state of mind that to treat it in that way, with that mixture of temerity and frivolity, with that lack of awareness and fear, was perfect folly. Which is not to say that it (French society) was itself very wise at the time." The coup d'état brought about by the *ordonnances* was inopportune; but the revolution did not deserve to succeed. These great events whose hopes he had shared as both a Saint-Simonian and a liberal provide him merely with the proof of their failure, the sign of a grave and miserable catastrophe.

It is noteworthy that in both 1830 and 1848, personal issues played a part in distancing Sainte-Beuve from the political hopes that he may have nurtured. Following the arrival of the citizen monarchy in 1830, the republicans at the daily *National* accuse him of betrayal for having written a sympathetic study of the royalist mystic Ballanche. They let him know that they are indignant and astonished. They express the disappointment of men of feeling. This incident shows the critic how a writer who wishes to remain true to himself should shun those groups who represent a different set of values. "In that situation," he wrote, "I gained insights which were very useful to me about the partisan spirit, and about how little there is to be gained, for true men of letters and for critical minds, from mingling with political groups, which are always more or less intolerant; because one is obliged, on one side or the other, to form a view and hence to willingly close off entire perspectives for one's intelligence." In 1848, the antagonism is more serious. Having discovered his name on the civil list, his friends in power accuse him of having been in the pay of the previous government. He has no difficulty in justifying himself, but the bitterness he feels drives him more and more towards pessimism and indifference. As a critic he is a severe judge of governments, the revolutions that overthrow them and the new order that these revolutions found. As an artist, he turns away from all political involvement. These are the simple responses that the free exercise of self-examination always require of one.

Maxime Leroy offers a lengthy justification for Sainte-Beuve's decision to accept what happened on December 2 and rally to the Empire. He shows how his taste for authority, which developed under the influence of Saint-Simon, finds more to praise than to blame in the new regime. In 1839 he wrote in a letter that André Rousseaux quotes in his recent collection of critical articles, *The Classical World*: "The disorder continues, but what I am struck by is less a collapse of the regime, which is far less imminent, I believe, than logic would

indicate, less that, than the pitiful nature of this sort of government and society; the organized mediocrity, the enforced nul-
lification of people who could well prove themselves capable,
the triumph of haranguing and harassment over good honest
sense and the true way to lead men and govern States. Oh for
a man, no matter who, but damn it! a man who will one
day sit astride this society: how he'll avenge himself, and with
justification, and how he'll spur it on!"[2] He accepts that man
of authority out of weariness, a yearning for repose, and the
hope that a strong government will bring about the begin-
nings of a recovery, "a patched-up recovery," and because now
he is famous, he feels freer when he is offering adhesion without complacency than within the constraints of opposition.
There is a good deal of reserve and a certain disdain in the
political choice he makes, and what he says about it has all the
appearance of an ironic enigma, even today: "Wise and honest
minds," he writes, "who in normal times prefer the procedures
of liberty, have accepted the fact that during certain public
crises it is necessary to endure temporary dictators, and they
have rallied to these latter out of pure good sense, and a pressing awareness of the situation."

Charles Maurras, as we know, gave the name "organizing
empiricism" to the method of political observation practiced
by Sainte-Beuve, which led him, in a century consumed by
systems, ideology, abstract passions, and a frenzy of instinct,
to submit to the law of facts and results. That is the main
lesson provided by this circuitous, changeable mind, who was
religious deep down, uneasy and wounded, and over whom
intelligence, in conjunction with a sensibility that was constantly in search of harmony, exercised an all-embracing and
limitless sway. The inventing of regimes, the perfecting of the
imaginary or the creating of combinations are all practices that
reading Sainte-Beuve tends to drive from our minds. He does
not humiliate reason, but he rescues it from the reign of theory
where it would gladly settle, and defines its fundamental goals
as political ones, namely convenience, utility, and the pursuit

of means. In Sainte-Beuve there is neither doctrine, nor constitutional plan, nor dogmatic fantasy. If he criticizes Prévost-Paradol for his faith in parliamentary democracy, this is because he sees it as a system that claims to satisfy too vast a range of hopes, and an abstract solution to which historical diversity cannot be adapted. What should be asked of a government? he asks. That it provide "a certain number of generations with peace and happiness, as they understand those terms." And what then? Further adjustments will be made, if needs change, that is to say if as a repercussion of a war, an industrial innovation or a philosophy, the old molds break. "Forms come and go, they disintegrate, they are transformed." Should one complain about this, out of wounded pride? No: one should accept it. Such are the ways of a world to which the mind imparts experience.

It goes without saying that the limits of such realism cannot easily be tolerated. Sainte-Beuve himself did not tolerate them. He constantly broke free of them, and carried within him dreams that were awakened under the impulse of his stubborn beliefs. As a Saint-Simonian in his youth, he devoted part of himself to vague, consoling hopes, a sort of pious optimism that no disappointment could succeed in eliminating. The Goncourt brothers recalled the violence of one of his retorts at a dinner where someone called for the establishment of literary rights in perpetuity: "Literary property should no more exist than any other sort," said Sainte-Beuve. "There should be no property. Everything should be renewed, everyone should take his turn at working." That is the spontaneous response of a mind that is remote from facts, suddenly turned in on itself and more eager to defend a personal ideal than a general order of things as expressed through observation. In this way, the law that the abbé Brémond sought to bestow on him in his book *The Novel and the History of a Conversion* abjures itself and then withdraws along the pathways of an obscure soul in which disquiet, disappointment, and the urge to love—impulses that are constantly thwarted—sustain a dissatisfaction which inspires his investigations, but makes him secretly destroy the tranquil realism to which he is attached.[3] One of Sainte-Beuve's most significant texts has been singled out by Victor Giraud:[4] "You see," we read in a letter to George Sand, "I was a rather feminine nature; I find it difficult to focus on things in themselves, though I do make an effort; but when it comes to things personified in a living being, I would gladly have believed in them, and with a faith which would have asked nothing better than to be a lasting one."

It must also be noted that Sainte-Beuve's empiricism, his concern for facts, and the enlightened obedience he shows them tend to encourage in him an almost desperate view of society and of people. His observations, says Maxime Leroy, give the impression that society is a force that is almost totally blind. Ideas have no influence over it. It can neither be changed nor reformed. The rare suggestions afforded by study and experience are significant only for their modesty, and it is in an almost futile combat against inexorable historical forces and the workings of self-interest, against stupidity and blindness, that politicians deploy their wisdom, and the more they are aware of the feeble extent of their action and the poverty of their means, the more capable they are of acting. In this sense, Sainte-Beuve's empiricism is the expression of a spiritual attitude whose anguished nature is unmistakable. It is natural to invoke in his case, as Leroy does, the strange retreat of the abbé Sieyès, who, driven by disillusion, renounced everything that he was and withdrew into silence. Thus it is that extreme incredulity, once reconciled with itself, leads to a desperate clarity that forbids all distraction, makes the possession of any treasure mere vanity, and finally effaces the night.

—March 10, 1942

Stories of Childhood

Writers naturally allow themselves to be tempted by memories of their childhood and to derive from what they remember about it works that appear to them to be spontaneously poetic. The German Romantics and some of the French Surrealists sought in childhood the elements of a mythic frame of mind in which dream, imagination, and sentiments of an ambivalent kind brought forth a powerful reality that was linked to a transfiguration of the past. But endeavors such as these are possible only if there is a harmony between the gift of total spontaneity and a solemn awareness of the world, and after so many famous works that have prolonged either their success or their failure, these endeavors can be renewed only if profound personal experience can equip itself with the means that a free art provides. If that is not the case, rather than the resources he had hoped for, the childhood from which the writer draws his themes will supply him with all the inelegance of a genre that is conventional precisely because it turns purity and absence of artifice into a commonplace.

Of the two stories of childhood that have recently been published, one avoids the defects of the genre by refusing its

ambitions, while the other succumbs to those defects so completely that it provides what amounts to an exemplary version
of them. *Just Like Children* by Marc Bernard is a book of rare
quality in which everything is simple, but where things emerge
in a light that is invariably strange.[1] It appears possible to
praise this work in the serenest terms, and this epithet is by
no means unjustified. In Marc Bernard's work there is a sincere and radiant image of life, a precise estimation of people,
and a strict concern for what is true about them, just as in his
talents there is a capacity for generosity and sympathy which
discovers within the basic mediocrity of things a sense of their
authentic value. But at the same time, this gift for being everywhere on an equal footing with what is true is accompanied
by something quivering and vibrant whose significance is
complex. Though an ardent confidence and a knowing ingenuity have brushed aside the detritus of the world that we
enter, retaining only images of it that have undergone an exor-
cism, we perceive it also as the site of a tragic truth whose
outline can only be delineated by an absence of all bitter feeling or grief-stricken allusion. There is a benign affection here
that, far from concealing shadows and obliterating what is
cruel and harsh, makes their presence almost unbearable
through the silence in which it is content to dwell.

Marc Bernard's child lives on the outskirts of Nîmes, and
his mother is a seamstress. He lives the free life of the street,
and the street belongs to him. It is there that he learns the
ways of the world; he witnesses scenes that he understands and
that do not inflict any premature wounds on him. Having got
the measure of the experiences offered by the town, when his
mother becomes the cook in a chateau he discovers the serene
freedom of grassy plains and a life of rustic roving. Then he
goes back to the streets. A brawl between cutthroats, the violent death of a murdered couple, and images of his affection
for his mother are among the episodes that form the story of
his youth. He moves in Protestant circles and attends a Catholic school. He succumbs to a violent religious crisis just as he

takes his first communion. Finally, he takes up an apprentice-ship. He is twelve; the book of his childhood is finished.

It is clearly not enough to admire this story of a wretched childhood simply because it is sober and free of declamatory sentiment. It would be more appropriate to establish how the child's memories of a difficult life succeed in preserving all of the radiant aspects that belong to youth, without toning down its harsh realities. This would reveal that the transfiguration that memory allows does not entail surrounding all the humble facts of everyday existence with the shadow of happy or unhappy feeling, but imagining a new perspective on them in which the truth of the detail does not change, but where the exceptional character of certain moments is brought out. This is what makes Marc Bernard's story so remarkable. It is made up of episodes that are perfectly ordinary in themselves yet appear to have unprecedented import. The slimmest anecdotes attract the reader as if they were the reflection of some unique and poignant truth. This is because that was how they were during childhood, or at least that is how memory associates them with the inaccessible memory of the earliest emotions. One or two brilliant images, composed not of elements taken from a distorted reality but of a reality that has been clasped by a free and eager sensibility, form the points that compose a glorious constellation. And poverty itself seems like splendor while remaining simply poverty, but within this misfortune, accepting it for what it is, the violent vigor of a child's sensibility shines and burns in a series of brilliant figures.

Marc Bernard was no less inspired when he decided to use what is true about the grown man he now is in order to throw light on the impressions of his youth. And similarly, he was certainly right to attach sophisticated and complex thoughts to his earliest experiences. Unthinking readers may be tempted to ask: how can the feelings of a child possibly correspond to something so well thought out? How can an ignorant sensibility be credited with an emotion that only a network of notions available to a mature mind can account for? But the opposite

would in fact be harder to believe. From the moment the
writer decided to turn back toward himself, and provide a
picture of things and people that would not betray them nor
conflict with the vision of a ten-year-old, yet would at the
same time be much more developed and coherent than it,
which is to say exactly the way that vision could have been
had he started out with a reference to one or two childhood
impressions and complemented these with observations made
later on—from that moment he could do nothing other than
seek to portray his childhood soul with the same sort of harmony, by explaining what he was then in the light of what he
has since become. The result is an art that is perfectly natural,
with a naturalness that one is content not to ask the author to
justify because one is fully aware that it is the outcome of
perfect stylization, and that to be faithful to its model con-
sisted first of all in discovering the truth of that model. It is
undoubtedly this horizon of truth, something like an infinitely
solemn and significant background, that increases the value of
these memories and restores them to a universe where they
display all of their significance. This impression can partly be
conveyed by saying that Marc Bernard talks of the woes of the
"humble," of what is tragically mean and miserably banal
about them, as if he had acquired a superior freedom in
relation to them, but also as if that freedom, that possibility
for frank, upright, and complete judgment had only been
achieved after tremendous efforts. What does it cost a writer
to be natural and truthful, when this naturalness and truthful-
ness are linked to the world that is most intimately his? That
is the question the following lines oblige us to confront, while
leaving us with a perfect image of what is authentic about *Just
Like Children*:

> I spent my childhood watching my mother, flamboyant in her
> wretched dress; she would wave her arms above her head, striding
> round the kitchen, brooding interminably over her misery, turning
> on the furniture and scolding it, on people, or even God. Was every-
> thing our enemy therefore? I made timorous progress. Only very

slowly did I see horizons open and high walls part, and the world cease to appear filled with desperation but rather be on offer; my shoulders broadened, I broke out of that shell which had kept me isolated. And today I still perhaps keep in the bottom of my heart some of the anguish of my childhood, which sometimes makes me shrink back fearfully, feel ashamed at being me or refuse to accept myself, as though a host of dead people were weighing down on my shoulders to prevent me from standing up straight. Those are values which I feel unable to applaud.

Agatha of Nieul l'Espoir by Odette Joyeux belongs in that series of works that are most perfectly epitomized by Jean Cocteau's *The Children of the Game*, and which tend to delve far enough into the ice-cold depths of childhood for innocence and purity to encounter crime and deceit there as their blameless symbol.[2] The pitfalls involved can be daunting. Odette Joyeux's heroine is a little girl of twelve who one day, during a circus performance, causes the death of an acrobat by disturbing a difficult balancing act with her cries. The accident throws the village into turmoil, and henceforth the little girl is associated with the idea of something extraordinary. This turns her into an alarming and enchanted character in the eyes of her young sisters. She herself is condemned to live a life of rapture and deceit in which there are only phantoms, impenetrable secrets and blood-soaked dreams. The years go by, but the enchantment endures. What was just play becomes a challenge to normal life; now the adventure must become real, and the novel ends in a whirlwind of crime, incest and suicide, which are the shadows cast across the adult world by a childhood that did not let go of its truth in time.

What makes a book like this stand out is not the story itself, the arbitrary aspects of which could have done with being toned down somewhat, but rather the fact that the story fails to find the level where it might have acquired a degree of authenticity. There is neither reality nor unreality in it; neither dream as a reality, nor reality made the subject of dream. Fantastical verisimilitude is as absent as the verisimilitude of things that truly are. At no time do we have the sense of a true fiction, but at no time either are we given the impression that the story is seeking to pass itself off as false. In fact, this story is so gratuitous that we see it neither as possible nor as impossible, and as we read on from one episode to the next, our hope is that we will encounter as many conventional features or borrowings from the stock-in-trade of poetic fairytales as possible, so that an air of parody that would not be without its charm may at least provide some underlying stability.

Odette Joyeux makes the mistake of yielding to her own effortless gifts and to the agreeable task of inventing a mode in which everything can be said gracefully, in a genre where what is required is precisely the severest sort of control, the strictest and most determined vigilance. It is not the reminiscences nor the puerile plot element nor the pretentiously false mythology that seem to condemn her book to a sorry fate; it is the neglect of what is necessarily implacable and harsh about the forms of a universe grounded in imagination. Here, what must be invented is a structure for reality in which everything that exists has meaning, and where even what has no meaning—that above all—needs to be justified in terms of the original invention. The most insignificant words and the simplest images at last acquire their full density, and their weight is so considerable that if the writer forgets to place them accurately, if he inserts them unthinkingly into his fictional system, that carelessness will be enough to cause the whole system to collapse, as can happen in a poem when two syllables clash prosaically. There is no more demanding taskmaster than the imagination. Hence the expression: obey your imagination, which is to say: you never lose your freedom more completely than when you are entirely your own prisoner.

—April 15, 1942

Jean Giono's Destiny

There are admirers of Jean Giono who are repelled by some of his books. They feel uneasy when they see such an instinctive writer turn deliberately in on himself and become a thoughtful theorizer. They say that the lyricism that illuminates his fictional work turns into a sort of bombastic sermonizing as a result of the reflective attention he pays it, and that the fine lights that burned without him seeing them are dismally extinguished once he tries to reflect them in a mirror himself. All of which goes to show how a great writer who is acknowledged for his evocative powers, and even his ability to get to the heart of things through his visionary eloquence, can nonetheless be denied the right to understand himself and express the meaning of what he does.

Such criticism can naturally find all sorts of reasons to justify it. It is normal that art should find its equivalent only in itself, and perish from any attempt to clarify it theoretically. It is normal too that an artist who no longer reflects on his work, but rather on himself, and who offers an interpretation of his existence that lays claim to general validity and either

condemns or glorifies an entire world, should suddenly suffer
blindness and be deprived of the light that his finest pages
once reflected. Such a regrettable eclipse would tend to prove
that even works that are not the straightforward product of
undemanding virtuosity, but are capable of addressing the
ultimate reason for things, nevertheless have only a literary
value, and cannot sustain the enquiring scrutiny that seeks to
identify a deeper issue within them.

Yet it is not easy, as people often do, to deny Jean Giono
purely and simply the intellectual and moral concerns that
represent for him what is serious about his life and his talent.
It is not by accident that he presumed to give himself this
prophetic mission, this evangelization that has allowed him to
attract numerous disciples, especially abroad. He is fundamentally predestined to be something more or something other
than a writer. If that means losing some of his luster, it still
does not permit him to evade what necessarily causes him to
lose it. He feels fundamentally obliged to pursue his possibilities to the utmost, and he can only do so by cutting himself
off from his true powers. He is entirely himself in his own
eyes when he is already no longer himself for others when they
judge his talent. He fulfills himself inwardly through a certain
impoverishment at the level of his art.

It is remarkable that a writer who is known above all for
being an instinctive one and an adversary of intelligence,
should be so deeply wedded to a task that, in certain respects,
has intellectual significance. It would appear that his mastery
of his art has encouraged him to make his great spontaneous
visions the object of almost exclusively theoretical reflections.
He has been unable to refrain from giving an account of himself, and in this process of self-understanding, he has been
unable to avoid the purely mental transposition and the
already highly unnatural version of himself constituted by the
sort of applied morality that he has made his own. Something
deliberate, which is to say artificial, comes from deep inside
him. It is not enough for him to write, he must also derive a

speculative and practical vision from what he writes. He observes himself with total awareness of what he is doing, and doubles back on himself in what is a highly dangerous contortion for someone who can declare: "I feel a perpetual need for total sincerity." And he is not satisfied with this disguise, since he feels the further need to use arguments in order to justify the authentic form of life that is his, and which finds expression in his work. He needs to prove what for him is totally natural, and to strip it of what is natural as a result, transforming it into an occasion for calculations, doubts and intelligible processes. What has happened to the apotheosis of instinct here, and what has become of sincerity? To be sincere in this case is to know that one is sincere, just as to provide proof of the fact is to have brilliantly ceased to conform to it.

And so in his new book, *The Triumph of Life*, Jean Giono returns to a project he has already presented in *True Riches*, and through a mixture of reverie, evocation, guided fiction and arguments from example he attempts to bring to light the profound significance of a certain way of life, and of the world which makes that life possible.[1] This work is decked out in the finest colors and shot through with extraordinary beauties, and it appears much more skillfully constructed from a theoretical point of view than the one it complements. It would be quite unfair to dismiss it from this point of view alone, by seeing in it merely a defense of craftsmanship and a heavy-handed indictment of the modern world, the civilization of the machine and the decadent condition of a humanity that has lost touch with itself, as if Jean Giono had been content to entertain the most banal assertions and then make them the essence of what he has to reveal. As well as areas of light and shade that transform its more mediocre perspectives, his book contains an effort that reflects the ambiguity of his destiny and an image of the shifts and slides of a mind that is at odds with itself.

If one were to try and provide an analysis of his theories, the task would be as basically ridiculous as attempting to translate into abstract formulas the figures of his poetic vision. Nevertheless, it is possible to trace the clash of a number of themes that allow us to get a better idea of what such traditionally simple ideas as the flight from the city and the return to the fields signify for him. There is no doubt that for the author of *The Joy of Man's Desiring*, contact with the earth was an almost mystical experience.[2] In the solitude of natural time and space he experienced an anxious rapture, a torpid giddiness that led him to believe that he was at one with the universe, and it is that knowledge, extricated from the forms of everyday life and as unrelated to action as it is to rational analysis, whose mysterious intoxication he has sought to express in a number of very fine books.

> Mixed in with the panic magma (and even more intimately than I have been able to say) I have shared in every life. I have truly felt that I was without boundaries. I am a mixture of trees and animals and elements, and the trees and animals and elements that surround me are made out of me as much as out of themselves. I have discovered for myself an immense bodily and spiritual joy. Everything bears me, everything supports me, everything carries me off.

What he finds in this great communion with nature is thus a certain way of approaching the absolute, and the "triumph of life" expresses this ecstatic movement, far removed from all the rules of banal existence that the modes of action and abstract intelligence require.

Precisely insofar as it defies the claims of knowledge and occupies a totally different level, such experience cannot be contested. For the person who undergoes it, it is of inexpressible value, and it lies beyond the reach of those critiques and justifications on which it is quite incapable of calling for assistance. To seek out its whys and wherefores, to found it even on the best motives there are, is to transform it entirely and transfer it from a universe where it holds absolute sway into a configuration where it is merely nonsense, or even worse, of mediocre significance and vulgarly utilitarian. Yet this degradation is precisely what Jean Giono accepts and organizes almost constantly. He has no hesitation about making a modest case for this overwhelming reality, in which reasons of convenience play an important part and invite agreement at the most practical level. He is happy to recommend the life of the peasant or the craftsman, which is to say something which for him constitutes an extraordinary symbol, because that life appears to him as the most rational and robust life possible, the only life that not even a planetary catastrophe could put an end to. He extols it for being peaceful and logical. He invites others to share it for the sorts of reasons that make people choose an honest trade that will set them up in life. And even if he thinks he has got to the bottom of things, embracing a system of proofs that can apply to an entire civilization, he continues to defend what is inexpressible with a well-ordered series of arguments, and to spread his net beneath what is only conceivable when it is in free fall and caught inside the harrowing turmoil of risk. It is not the weaknesses of his reasoning that should provoke outrage, but the deliberate slide from profound experience toward an order of concerns where every reason is feeble and where action annexes everything and renders it trivial.

It is likely that a similar spirit of confusion lies behind the passion for security and the desire for the quiet, stable life that Giono portrays when he evokes the things of the earth. Nothing could be more unlike the panic that he constantly holds up as his "diamond key" than this sense of repose. He himself has expressed the anguish that accompanies "the icy presence of the god":

> I was no longer searching for the path, I was the search itself, like both the ploughshare and the furrow. I penetrated deeper and deeper into the undergrowth; into that fearful mass of living matter. . . . Life was sucking me down so thoroughly into its midst, while offering neither death nor mercy, that sometimes like a god I felt that my head, my hair and my eyes were filled with birds, that my arms were heavy with branches, my chest swollen with goats, horses and bulls,

my feet dragging along roots, and the terror of primitive man made me bristle like a sun.

But out of this giddiness, farther than which it would seem impossible to fall, out of this rapture that is an abyss that opens endlessly beneath the feet, practical reason, which can only understand an experience like this in terms of its own world where everything is a goal, an end or a limit, creates a perfect image of repose, expressing the confident certainty that if one holds firmly to the earth, every difficulty will be resolved, every anxiety dispelled, and life will be definitively secured against the abyss. The ground is henceforth simply the calm assurance that keeps the modern forms of wretchedness and despair at bay.

Jean Giono appears to have hesitated for a long time before extracting from his own experience, linked as it is to what is most intimate within him, a general example which is valid not just for others but for all others. In his first books we see him refuse, out of extreme individualism, the collective enthusiasm presupposed by every version of the return to the land, even if it is a poetic one. In *True Riches* he could still write: "Have I found joy? No . . . I have found my own joy." And *The Triumph of Life* is, in certain of its pages, a paean to a solitary combat for which no one else can offer assistance, which permits him neither to husband his strength nor resort to mechanical means, and which is lost both if the task is too easy or the victory too perfect. He writes,

> No law can prevent men from showing individuality. However convergent the angles of vision from which they all look at the same object together may be forced to be, these angles form separate peaks in each soul. That is why men can bring something to life, in which case life gives back to them, for each time, they bring something that only they have the power to bring: their personal expression, and it is as a result of this that they have a reason to live.

It is also for this reason that Giono felt entitled to overcome his reserve, and in order to remind mankind of what is unique and personal about itself, to impose on it a vision that seemed valid for him alone. This attitude is perhaps not as contradictory as it appears. Mystics themselves, having made contact with the incommunicable, sometimes turn toward the world in order to teach it that there is something that cannot be communicated. In the same way, Giono makes his aspiration towards individual existence the condition and the means of a great project for general solidarity and universal fellowship. He who could write, I have found my own joy, not just joy, also writes: "My joy will endure only if it is the joy of everyone. When I am feeling wretched, I cannot find relief behind the murmurings of genius." That is the misfortune of an art that cannot be content with what it is. It understands that it is the reflection of a wondrous light that it cannot grasp directly. But in order to lift the veil on the star it has glimpsed in all its radiance, it must renounce its marvels, which seem merely a vain mirage, and henceforth it will offer nothing to the eye save a dim lamp that every ray of light has abandoned.

—May 6, 1942

The Revelation of Dante

Dmitry Merezhkovsky, who died a few months ago, left behind a number of posthumous works whose publication will serve to prolong his bizarre existence. In France we are quite familiar with the fate of this tormented writer, whom exile imbued with a dark, prophetic instinct and who found in the certainties of his revelation a source of indefatigable labor. Despite the breadth of his knowledge and the powerful organization of his intellect, he often seemed to lack seriousness, to be a mind eaten up by stubborn ideas, and deprived of any real audience less because what he said appeared absurd than because he would repeat himself on the subject of what is unique and turn any subject into an opportunity to repeat himself. That is one of the characteristics of a man with a message. He delivers it by becoming its prisoner. He gives permanent shape to a symbolic image of the future, so as to convince the present of it and familiarize the present with it. He turns what for him is enigma and allegory into immediately accessible truth. In the end, people take him at his word; he is no longer understood because he has obliged people to understand him too precisely.

Dante, which has been translated by Jean Chuzeville and has recently come out, does not entirely avoid that impression of an implacable return to the same point which so many of Merezhkovsky's works convey.[1] One has the feeling, and it is a distressing one in human terms, that certain myths, certain images, certain expressions without which his thought would not exist, return at regular intervals like leitmotifs whose repetition would seem to be necessary for his mental survival. At the heart of each of his reflections there reappears that assertion of Trinitarian revelation and eternal Scripture with which he defiantly challenges Goethe, that "demon of European culture." He needs to draw from each text and each significant life an arrow that points the way for his great pronouncements. This is the mark of an explosive obstinacy that is sometimes so extraordinary that it seems to be linked not just to the urgency of his testimony, but also to the singular structure of his intellect. It conjures up a mind that could think only by constantly reaffirming itself.

The passion with which Merezhkovsky took on the gravest of missions, and the anxiety for the wretched fate of mankind that took shape in the midst of all his hopes, give all of his works a feverish brilliance that his art was always careful to protect. Though it is unlikely to add much to everything we may already know on this great subject, his *Dante* nevertheless restores genuine significance, through its distortions and its prejudices, to a figure who is all too often obscured by his literary fame. He restores to him his destiny as a prophet, and establishes him alongside Luther as the greatest reformer of modern times. He seeks beneath his ponderous glory the oft-hidden light that has traversed abysses and foretells of days to come. He attempts to remove the veil beneath which the loftiest of poets appears in all the poetic supremacy that came from wielding a power that lay outside of poetry. Perhaps his prophetic urge makes him lose sight of Dante's true greatness, by encouraging him to use it as a symbol in which everything he holds dear is to be found. But the *Divine Comedy* can bear even an excess of admiration, and it willingly consents to being a haven for superior thoughts and grand desires that are not entirely its own. It is impossible to lend it more than it gives.

This study of Dante belongs to a series of works that are part-critical, part-religious, and part-poetic, and in which, going from East to West, Merezhkovsky consulted the great intellectual and spiritual witnesses of human life: Saint Augustine, Joan of Arc, Saint Theresa of Avila, Saint John of the Cross, Luther, Calvin, Saint Theresa of Lisieux, Dostoyevsky, and Tolstoy. For his mind, this enquiry signifies what the quest of the last man would be if, conscious of the cataclysm that is about to overtake civilization, he sought to rediscover the unity of spiritual experience, in order to bear witness to it for the last time, and reveal in tracks already half-erased the first signs of a reemerging path. To him, the contemporary world appears tragically doomed to collapse because, in his terms, it is the prisoner of the number two. This number is the symbol of war, of the endless opposition that pits man against God, flesh against spirit, the world below against the world above, the poor against the rich and peoples against each other as if they were all the bitterest of enemies. Everywhere there are twos, and between them, a mortal rivalry. "Alas!" says Goethe's Faust, "there are two souls within my breast, one yearns to be separate from the other, one clings to the earth in a surge of rough passion, while the other violently shakes off the dust and flies up toward the kingdom of its sublime ancestors." This tragedy in which man becomes divided in order to retreat from himself is the tragedy of the doomed world. He will have to descend like Dante into the depths of the abyss in order miraculously to reemerge.

With the vigor of inspired foresight, Merezhkovsky announced the end of this cataclysm by assembling the elements of an ancient revelation, that of Joachim of Fiore. In his view, if the number two is the sign of ruin, the number three, the three in one, the Trinity, is, as Dante puts it, "the principle of all miracles." The Russian writer places all of his hopes in a third kingdom of the Spirit, which will coincide with the reconciliation of the Christian East and West and be symbolized by the Church of Saint John. "It is John," he writes, "who will put an end to the 'great dispute' which extends across the ages and among peoples; the two separate halves of the Christian West—the two Churches, Catholic and Protestant—will be united by the orthodoxy of the past, which is not that of the present but that of the future, the Church of John in the third testament of the Spirit." Merezhkovsky pursued with tireless intellectual agility the solemn affirmation of this Apocalypse, in which the ambitions of Catholic traditionalists are distorted by Russian yearnings. In addition to his splendid vision of the Trinity triumphant, "three circles of three colors making a single one," Dante equips Merezhkovsky for this bizarre evangelization with a few snippets on which the Russian commentator seizes with his imperious ingenuity. In the twelfth canto of *Paradiso*, alongside Saint Augustine, Saint Hugh, Saint Victor, and several others, Saint Bonaventura shows Dante "brother Joachim of Calabria, blessed with the spirit of prophesy," the very same person who, after the second, new Testament, foretold that there would come "the Third, the Eternal Gospel of the Holy Spirit." This is just a step away from believing that Dante himself shares this belief, and for a man inspired that step is easily taken. The axis around which all of the *Divine Comedy* revolves would thus appear to be a second Pentecost, where the name of the Holy Spirit is identical in the first canto of the *Inferno* to that of the mysterious greyhound, that "Veltro" who must destroy the pitiless she-wolf. Veltro appears as a cryptogram of "the Eternal Gospel" of Joachim of Fiore: Vang ELeTeRO, and lends its heraldic emblem to the revelation of the Spirit. Merezhkovsky concludes from this that if the visible body of the *Divine Comedy*—its theological skeleton—comes from Saint Thomas Aquinas, its soul, its secret inspiration, was given to it by Saint Joachim of Fiore and expresses the hope of a new redemption without which the universe can only perish.

This struggle with enigmas does not blind Merezhkovsky to those points of brilliance that resist his interpretation. There is Dante, he says, but there is also an anti-Dante. And the anti-Dante is the Dante of the *Monarchy* and the *Banquet*, which set out a theory of a divided world split between two kingdoms, the Church and the State, whose unity is impossible. He is also the man who, spied on by the spotted panther, the *lussuria*, momentarily refuses to choose between Beatrice and the Prostitute and accepts a life torn by conflicting sentiments. Finally, he is perhaps the lover of Beatrice, in that by resigning himself to the principle of courtly love he appears to condemn the world of the flesh and prefer fiction to reality, play to action and the refinements of decadence to marriage. Deep down, however, Merezhkovsky does not seriously believe that for Dante love consists of this heresy: to love is not to love. On the contrary, he brings to light with a fine passion the admirable secret of Beatrice, which unites her ideal presence in heaven with the dreams of her earthly incarnation, and reconciles love here below with love on high. Perhaps Beatrice even declared her love for Dante before she died, as is suggested by these allusive lines from the *Vita Nuova*, one of the two keys to the life and the work according to Merezhkovsky: "And despite the fact that it would be fitting for me to say how she left us, I refuse to speak of it . . . because I lack the words to say it . . . and also because, if I said it, I would find myself compelled to boast." Why does Merezhkovsky attach such significance to the hypothesis of this supreme confession? Because in it he sees proof of the reality of love, and that real love is a principle of salvation. That is the Slavic face of this dispassionate prophesying. Christianity must be reconciled with life, disembodied sainthood set aside and heaven and earth held in a single embrace. Just as for Dostoyevsky earthly mystery must come into contact with the mystery of the stars, so according to the eternal Gospel Christianity must no longer signify a renunciation of the earth, but a new fidelity and a new love.

These strange thoughts, which are exceptional only because of the part-religious, part-intellectual form they take, and

which manifest the great themes of Russian consciousness—
the deep sense of division, the desperate effort at synthesis, the
devotion to Christianity, the refusal of Christian steadfastness,
the belief that the world is going to end, the belief in a new
world, the advent of a universal orthodoxy; these fantasies,
pursued with considerable erudition and in a feverish dialectic,
did not put Merezhkovsky in a position to say anything at all
about the work of Dante considered as poetic revelation. He
devotes only a few allusive pages to that subject, in an attempt
to discern the power of an art that drew its harmony from
symbol. "Dante," he writes, "is a great dreamer; his dream
continues for half a century. Inferno, Purgatory, Paradise. . . .
His entire work can be said to be nothing other than a symbolic, dreamlike prophesy." He observes also that all of
Dante's great visions: that of the *Vita Nuova* in which he sees
a naked person, wrapped in a cloth of blood that is devouring
his heart, the dream of the infernal forest, the image of the
"grand old man of Crete" and the revelation of the last five
cantos of *Purgatory*, are all frescoes from an interminable
dream that reflect an inner experience akin to that of ecstasy.
Allegory itself—and almost no other poet can permit such a
remark—has the transparent rigor and the crystalline logic
that are born of a nocturnal imagination whose secret remains
hidden from it; it is like day that conceals night, and the eye
that believes it has found a meaning there eventually becomes
lost in an inexhaustible reality. "Reader, sharpen well your
eyes here on what is true, for the veil is now so fine that you
could easily pass right through it." It is this vision capable of
transforming the original secret of things into an indestructi-
ble world that is absent from Merezhkovsky's personal revelation. Thought is revealed there in its nakedness, yet the only
mirror it encounters is that of fever. The bizarre, far from
being the deep-seated insignia of dream, appears as the flaw in
an intelligence that has failed to get the better of its shadows.

—May 13, 1942

Three Novels

Here are three novels of varying length and value, all three of them the work of writers who are still young, and linked by common concerns and almost identical defects. It is quite striking that all three novels seek to portray a certain form of human distress, and attempt to express it without resorting to the methods of ordinary psychology. It no less remarkable that they are all drawn toward the easy solution and are overwhelmed or at least held back by convention.

By its form, its internal rigor, and its outstanding qualities as a novel, *The Apprenticeship of the City* by Luc Dietrich is far superior to many run-of-the-mill works today.[1] It is by a writer who is already on top of his form, and whose intentions are often far-reaching. If it can be compared to *The Admission* by Julien Blanc or *Manly Solitudes* by Elizabeth Porquerol, which attract the eye less convincingly, it is because it bears the mark of the same ambitions, and despite its merits, is compromised by the same lack of rigor.[2] It is tempting to examine how, while employing such different means, these works all stumble at the same point on their ascent so that, even when successful, they resemble each other through the way they fail.

All three novels take as their subject the misfortune of a man who, in the course of numerous experiences, seeks to overcome his wretched condition and in doing so, aggravates the causes of the disorder that is his lot. What is striking is that not one of these three characters displays a failing that is either peculiar to him, or can simply be put down to collective injustice. The wretchedness of each wretched individual is an indictment neither of his character nor of society. Even in *The Admission* or *Manly Solitudes*, where there is a certain amount of political description, it is not possible to reduce the story of these misfortunes to a settling of scores between an oppressed individual and a corrupt society. Why do these beings endure their distress so obscurely, and why do they go from adventure to adventure like blind men who only gradually become aware of their route? It is because they are cowards, and because their cowardice reflects a state of impoverishment that no particular cause can lay bare.

Of the three, Luc Dietrich's hero is the one least given to making demands and most inclined to consider himself responsible for his misfortune. His story begins during a brawl in which he is wounded, then given assistance for his wound by a young woman who mysteriously comes to his rescue. From this moment on he opts for the easy life, and surrendering to this assistance whose tainted character he tolerates without compunction, he evasively accepts everything such a life can bring him, until one day, he wrecks it out of innate obduracy, Schadenfreude, and secret disquiet. This is the beginning a new period of wandering which leads him from hunger to love, from requited love to unrequited love, from missed opportunities to abandoned chances. The detail of these adventures does not matter. The hero rejects what he finds, demands what escapes him, exploits what he has and goes in search of what he does not have in a state of confusion where he seesaws endlessly between insufficiency and excess. His attempts at self-discipline are initially no more than a naive reflection of his disordered state. He is the victim of what is vague about both his despair and his destiny.

The subject of the book is apprenticeship, and that is also the theme of the other two books. Dietrich's character experiences an inner impoverishment into which he sinks relentlessly, but he discovers too by what means salvation can be achieved. He gradually learns to know himself, and imposes an order on himself that protects him against what he lacks. What is he? Someone who gets everything mixed up, who can make no headway through his chaos, who dissipates himself and spreads himself thinly, who bursts his banks and whom nothing can contain. Even when he throws off the yoke of an immoral stroke of good fortune and freely condemns himself to poverty, he is merely flailing about inconsistently, and seeking in evasiveness and lies a pathway to personal oblivion. The last chapter of the novel is entitled "The Honeypot." This is because the wretched hero has discovered the reasons for his misfortune, and has decided to play the honeypot no longer, "the sort that spills its contents onto the tablecloth, a dress or the carpet, its exquisite, perfumed, sugary content, which makes hands sticky, drips into shoes, and sticks in the hair." His discipline will require him henceforth to make something of himself and contain himself, to deprive himself in order to receive, and to abjure in order to be. His last act is to take leave of someone he loves, because he sees everything that lies between him and the person he would need to be in order truly to love her.

The idea behind *The Admission* and *Manly Solitudes* is much more chaotic, but it too reflects the adventurous quest of two individuals as they laboriously strive for liberation. In the part-unreal, part-indeterminate world that provides the main interest of the novel, Julien Blanc's Le Vignaise is caught in a struggle between cowardice, the tyranny of corrupt institutions, and the peculiarities of sentiment which afflict him; he is weak, and his lapses make him weaker by the day. He is proud and wretched, solitary yet incapable of solitude, corrupted by what he likes and saved from corruption by suffering. All of that portrays a rather nebulous distress, whose infantile character is revealed through a series of long bombastic speeches. Eventually, this hapless young man also finds salvation and is "admitted" into the realm of what is human from which his failings have distanced him hitherto, but to which they have also brought him close. The seal of that higher blessing which misfortune is rarely deprived of is bestowed upon him. All's well that ends well, therefore, in these destinies that are drawn to the abyss and seem marked out for catastrophe. If the young hero of *Manly Solitudes* also goes through periods of oppression, degrading experiences and a withdrawal into himself from which his mediocre success provides no relief, he endures these unfortunate episodes only so as to attain what is purest, and here the example of a great artist who was also condemned and also saved accompanies him like a memory of indelible human hope.

One wonders why three novels that are so different in tone and development yet so similar in intent, should all be predominantly concerned with a search for the happy ending which each of them deems essential. This is obviously not just a straightforward novel convention, designed to ensure a satisfactory outcome after a series of rather too gloomy episodes. It is the work itself that, from one failure to the next, from ruin to defeat, hastens toward the providential conclusion that it is exclusively designed to produce, and that also makes it appear arbitrary and false. It is as if, having descended into a narrow pit from which they feared they would never emerge, the authors had had only one thing in mind: to find a way out at all costs, to achieve redemption within an anxious situation that in itself could only signify that there was no way out, no redemption possible. This inflection is especially noticeable in Luc Dietrich's book, because he devotes more space to the description of a wretched state in which a spirit of frivolity, natural listlessness, and anxious agitation are all strangely combined. Why does his hero find salvation? Because he gives himself moral rules. His salvation takes place at the level of personal psychology. He discovers that by becoming a less impatient, more secretive, and more limited person, he will escape the temptations of delirium that almost destroyed him. This solution is not without interest it must be said, but let us be clear what sort of detour has made it possible. Dietrich's novel appears first of all as the novel of a man whose solitude and emptiness are not due in any way to his own defects, but to a deeper state of impoverishment. If he drifts miserably from good fortune to bad, it is because he has an inkling of a tragic truth on which he does not have the courage to dwell, but with which he does not want to sever all connection either. It is not because he is immoral, fickle, and dissolute that he appears to be constantly walking over an abyss; it is because he has had a vague revelation of the meaninglessness of contingent human affairs. At this level there is no hope of an optimistic conclusion. The book slowly pivots therefore, and as it gradually becomes the reassuring novel of a man whose disquiet and misfortune can be explained by his disorderly character, it ensures his deliverance by henceforth focusing solely on the errors of one particular individual destiny.

Luc Dietrich's book thus wavers between moral or psychological concerns and deeper, more concrete issues that he distinguishes only to betray them. In the same way, *The Admission* and *Manly Solitudes* mix together metaphysical anxiety, social recrimination, and sensual reverie in a highly infantile manner. Their wretched heroes go from being political accusers to becoming exhausted, moaning solitaries. They complain and they denounce themselves. They flit between their own misfortunes and the misfortunes of others, like will-o'-the-wisps that are scattered by the wind and do not even light up the marshland that sustains them. They are incapable of seeing anything whatever through to its conclusion. What are they? What do they represent? Security awaits them after the false solitude and mendacious distress whose badge they briefly wore, as they confused the vague murmurings of their own pretention with mortal torments. They are shadows that will be content with the shadow of a satisfaction.

As well as the optimistic mirage that surrounds these works of desperation, their common feature is provided by a set of those anecdotal clichés that are usually deployed in order to portray distress and degradation. These conventions, which became current in the naturalist novel, are curiously tenacious. It is strange that the symbol of debasement for the literary hero should remain drugs, venal love, or the corruption of luxury (in addition, Elizabeth Porquerol and Julien Blanc invoke the infamies of journalism and the shabbiness of politics). All these adventures are inspired by a moral conformism that makes their significance difficult to appreciate, and allows the feeling of anxiety that such a decline ought to inspire blur into indifference. No doubt we can comprehend the scruples of these desperate young people, who thrive on indulgent affection while vainly yearning for a purer experience of love; but the tragic sense of life has nothing to do with a liking for honesty, and it is difficult to take seriously a world whose abysses are represented by stories of drug-taking, and its summits by the ideals of a well-behaved young man.

These reservations apply particularly to *The Admission* by Julien Blanc, which combines a number of quite successful mythic inventions with a realist hodgepodge whose utterly negligent style brings out its conventional character even more starkly. In *Manly Solitude* another combination predominates, and a metaphoric impressionism in which images call forth other images thanks to pleasing affinities, alternates with an infantile naturalism whose vulgarity is both unconvincing and devoid of charm. *The Apprenticeship of the City* on the contrary boasts a solid, well-developed form. Luc Dietrich divides each of the parts of his book into a series of very short chapters, which allow him to move quickly from one piece of action to the next, and without interruption to mix in reverie with story, lyrical analysis with lean and furious description and facts with the thought that contests them and hones itself against them. In some episodes there is an icy indifference that saves them from being arbitrary, and restores to them a new authenticity made up of irony and disdain. In others, there is an unleashing of feeling during which vulgar detail is swept away by the passion that glories in it. The work as a whole allows us to forget the more facile inventions of detail, and the happy ending itself disappears in the ponderous, cumbersome, and anxious impression that constantly accompanies the wretched hero as he advances toward an empty ideal.

—May 20, 1942

After *Dangerous Liaisons*

Among its various qualities, Jean Blanzat's latest book displays that of appearing to be new thanks to the already time-honored conventions it employs. His *Morning Storm* is an epistolary novel.[1] It does not have a story. From among the set of processes that generally make up a work of fiction, and that includes, often haphazardly, narrative, dialogue, monologue, diary entries, and all the permutations of those simple forms, Jean Blanzat has selected only the most antiquated convention, and one that seemed most likely to plunge its reader back into the past. And with it, he has produced a singular, very pure and highly unconventional work.

It is impossible to think about this genre without recalling the page that Jean Giraudoux devotes to it in his study of Laclos,[2] and one of Blanzat's other merits is to have provided a satisfying illustration of those remarks, for which *Dangerous Liaisons* appears as the pretext and the sole justification. A writer who produces an epistolary novel has chosen to borrow from reality a convention that is already by nature a literary one. He employs a form of realism that does violence to realism. He depicts people at the moment of their everyday lives when they enter literature, exist only through the written word and renew their image of themselves and others thanks to the mirror which language provides. His choice implies the preliminary claim that we are only really the masters of our feelings, even at their most spontaneous, or our confidences at the point where they are just taking shape, through the medium of a well thought-out language and the highly revealing developments of a style. Realism for a novelist is in that case a matter of imitating a literature that is unreflecting in nature by means of a literature that is the fruit of calculation. It gives common rhetoric the extra level of dignity it required for it to become an art, but to which it aspired from the very outset.

Another characteristic of this curious literary form is that it presupposes the violence of a drama that it is banned from representing things directly. Jean Giraudoux has compared the success of *Clarissa*, *The New Héloïse*, or *Dangerous Liaisons* to that of a tragedy, which is to say their success rewarded the genre best able, in an age when tragedy was dying, to perpetuate its prestige. And the epistolary novel does not only resemble tragedy by its proud solemnity as it slowly develops according to the alternating rhythm of dialogue, or by the priority it grants to studied speech and restrained gesture in which spontaneity finds its true expression; it also resembles it through its concern to exclude any direct representation of action, which it allows in only by way of an indirect account or an allusive reference. In an epistolary novel the drama is never present. It is detectable only in the trace that it leaves on the narrator's sensibility. Its appearance takes the form of a moral commotion. It is the hollow imprint of events whose profile is perceptible only through this emptiness. It is all the more brutal and powerful for being split between several beings, who give voice to it and are the bearer of its discordant revelation each in their turn.

The genre presents analysis with the possibility of avoiding the cruder pitfalls of the psychological novel. Like the events, the characters exist only from the angle that they adopt in relation to themselves. What they say about themselves or about others is the expression of a state whose authenticity is revealed by the rest of those who witness it as continuously questionable. Each correspondent paints a picture of what he is which is not necessarily true in itself, and whose only truth is sometimes simply the fact that he is painting it. He portrays himself when he judges others, but this judgment provides a complete picture neither of him nor of those he judges, since the objective elements escape us, and we are caught in a growing web of uncertainties or conflicting accounts. Even if the primary goal of the novelist is not this indefinite flight from psychology taking place within psychology itself, he cannot avoid transforming every character into a momentary enigma, thanks to the convergent perspectives of the other characters and the air of affectation which accompanies even the least deceitful letter. Every epistolary novel contains psychologically the seeds of a plot in which the letters that are exchanged would be anonymous. Each person is elusive; the drama itself remains hidden. And it is in the unease generated by this multifaceted dissembling that it finally bursts onto the scene.

Morning Storm fulfills the requirements of the genre it has chosen thanks to the beauty of its form and the persistent purity of its language. The six correspondents and the letters they exchange express themselves with the most scrupulous care, and with a degree of superiority that gives each passion its true dignity. It is perfectly clear that these rather ordinary beings, who are very far from ranking themselves alongside the heroes of tragedy, can nevertheless only reach out to each other with the noblest of words, and by employing a language that rejects disorder, vulgarity, and harshness. They express themselves using only the most harmonious expressions. They translate their inner turmoil into terms whose rhythm and balance endow precision with a more intense insolence. They confess themselves in a vocabulary where all is reserve, reticence, and secrecy. What is more, they all speak the same language. The adolescent who is the hero of the book, the two girls who exchange confidences about him, the teacher who lectures him and the woman who seduces him all employ the same impeccable tone, the same relentlessly elevated way of speaking. What are we to think about such unity of form when it is extended to characters who are manifestly so varied? We may object to it in the name of realism, or see it as a convention whose effortlessness ends up being monotonous. But "in this mildly inflated language," as one of the characters puts it, "which is stilted and sustained by bombast," in this abstract solemnity from which they never deviate, it is also possible to hear an expression of the gravity which they have in common, a reminder of the elaborate tragedy into which the epistolary novel pours the sentiments of everyday life, so as to restore to them their literary authenticity.

The story of Jacques Tarentière is that of an adolescent who gives the impression of representing the misfortunes of adolescence with a degree of purity, awkwardness, and infantilism that allows them to appear as an expression of pride. His story is nonexistent, and he himself is a negligible quantity. He is merely a moment in his own existence, but this moment, because of its nonviable character and the state of apparent impossibility in which he experiences and lives it, takes on a dramatic significance which makes all those around him, even when they try to bring it down to more realistic proportions, feel more or less afraid. This young scholar, home for the holidays, suffering from yet also enjoying his unease and combining all the contradictions that together constitute youth, seems exclusively destined to plunge all the people he frequents into a state of embarrassment and maladjustment through his own arrogance, the considerable guile behind his awkward way of being, and the emanations of his inner agitation. He brings with him that additional quantity of arrogance and disorder thanks to which the most orderly exchanges in an unpretentious society become discordant; wherever he is to be found, the acoustic alters and voices go out of tune, echoing what is still the quaver in his own.

It is gratifying to think that the adolescent condition that, for the last twenty years, has allowed so many writers to produce complacent, undemanding books, can still provide the pretext for a work that is free of all false seduction, and even freer of those murky depths which seem to be inseparable from a subject of this sort. Not that some of Jacques Tarentières's letters are not objectionable for the implausibility of what they confess or the specious agitation of their form. Those are the ones whose lofty style is a vain attempt at imitating the feverish disorder of language, or else provides too direct a translation of experiences that are inexpressible. But these are few in number, and the general impression is one of a work that exploits its weaker moments so as to attain an authentic reality. Is it a fragmentary analysis in which the forms of an ill-defined state are seen from various angles? Is it a description by means of which the various witnesses to the drama take it in turns to express at random the images they perceive of it? Do they see clearly? Are they all mistaken? Is there anything in the observations to which the metamorphoses of this young adolescent give rise that can convey their truth? No one understands him, and yet these misunderstandings put together make up a faithful portrait.

Jean Blanzat has surrounded his novel with an aura of morality that could have altered its contours, but merely delineates them more precisely and with greater character. In this he again proves faithful to the conventions of the epistolary novel. When it is held up to the light so to speak, *Dangerous Liaisons* reveals the almost unbroken thread of a moralist's reflections. Laclos constantly adds his own remarks to those of his characters, keeping them separate through an imperceptible change of tone. In *Morning Storm*, a teacher has the task of expressing what maturity, culture, and pedagogical experience have to say about a state that is a challenge to maturity, knowledge, and thought. What is the misfortune of youth? It is reluctant to learn the art of resemblance. Ignorant of what exists, it turns that ignorance into a privilege that it refuses to relinquish. With others and with things it has random, stormy, and futile relations. It clashes with what it denies, and even that clash is unreal. It suffers, but finds suffering gratifying thanks to the feeling it provides that youth is unique, and the complacency that this feeling inspires. "Beware of the bottomless heart which is held up as an example to us," says the master to his pupil. "It is a cramped prison. No one ever enters it. The original inhabitant is deaf and dumb, and cannot allow anyone else inside. He does not even know what he is himself. Briefly anxious about his solitude, he pretends it is his joy. He is no longer a man, he is a permanently deserted place where feelings which nothing can ever connect together follow on endlessly from each other."

Critics who like to find in young authors the influence of the writers who preceded them will no doubt say that Jean Blanzat reminds then partly of François Mauriac and partly of Jacques Chardonne. From François Mauriac he appears to have inherited a predilection for the problems of adolescence, the fever that inflames them and the urge to express what is impure using what is pure. With Jacques Chardonne he shares a sort of moral inventiveness, the pleasure of varying the light by changing the perspective, a transparency that clouds the eye by drawing it into a substance that is infinitely clear. But these resemblances are no more than hypothetical points of reference. Jean Blanzat's book bears witness to an artistic experience combined with a moral one in which man, experienced as a mystery, tries to express himself through the abstract comparisons that, in our classical literature, have always made it possible to capture shadows. He can be criticized for not having pushed his work to the point of extreme conflict that the genre presupposes, for having given the primary roles to secondary characters and for making the central hero as it were his own confident, around whom the dramatic action drifts uneasily. But still he has the merit, which is worth just as much as the investigations of a profounder art, of having conveyed a state in which untruth and verbal aberration are essential in a language that speaks the truth, from which everything turgid and arid is banished, and that gives pure, clear resonance to the tragic mystifications of youth.

—June 17, 1942

The Misfortunes of Duranty

Duranty's fate provides an example of the misfortunes that can sometimes befall a writer. Almost forgotten today, already unrecognized during his lifetime, during which he struggled in vain after a form of art that he himself represented only equivocally, his gifts were greater than his achievements, and even the success that rewarded him for a few years does not seem to have reflected the true nature of his talent. Yet he was fortunate to have loyal friends. Baudelaire admired him. More than one attempt has been made to bring his works back into print, so that he should acquire the reputation he was unjustly deprived of. It may be that Jean Paulhan will have more luck than his precursors, and that the short study he has published as a preface to Duranty's first novel, *The Misfortune of Henriette Gérard*, will offer this luckless writer the chance he has waited for in vain for almost a century.[1]

The place that Duranty occupies in literary history would normally be enough to save him from oblivion. Unfortunately, his theoretical views merely led to an association with writers who were more mediocre than he was, and allied him with a genre whose discredit increased the more successful it became. He is of course one of the founders of realism in the novel. As is well known, around 1850 a number of new writers who were driven by an irresistible need to be different from their precursors discovered that the novel had been corrupted by excessive invention, and they sought to free it from the influence of the fantastic. Their concerns at least prove that in those days there was no misunderstanding about the meaning of Balzac's work, and that Balzac appeared, through his extraordinary talent for abstract creation, to have opened up the novel to the extravagances of the imaginary. The writers of 1850 no longer wish to be in competition with the registrar's office by creating imaginary beings who can pass for living people. They do not try to outdo reality; they imitate it, they copy it, and claim to take everything from it. Their wish—perhaps also their secret justification—is to be nothing but themselves, and to exist only as the reflection of everyone. They take a naïve pride and discover a guiding rule in their own impotence.

Naturally, it very soon becomes clear that the peremptoriness of realism is entirely due to its ambiguity. What is the real, what is "everyone"? In the journal he edits with Champfleury around 1856, Duranty has just one thing in mind: to combat Flaubert, who to his mind betrays the realist ideal through his bourgeois vision of things and his elitist literary tastes. The dual tendency that realism seeks to introduce into literature is clearly apparent in these years of political upheaval: a tendency to conflate reality with popular reality, and a mistrust for works of style. The novel must copy the real, and the real is not the society of the ruling classes, but the life we are familiar with from what happens in the street, from country scenes and family life. By endowing his observations and his language with a style, Flaubert is unfaithful to the art he thinks he is defending. He strays from what is natural, relying on words rather than documents; he encourages the writer to deform what exists rather than reproduce it without affectation.

The demands of realism were naïve rather than new, as was already obvious in the nineteenth century to readers of Restif de la Bretonne. But did Duranty have any inkling of this? Did he see that the problems he raised were leading him down a tortuous path where imperious theoretical claims were of little use? He wrote only three novels, and after the second one, *Fine William's Cause*, he even remained silent for ten years.[2] Jean Paulhan, who points out the disadvantages of realism and indeed the whole drama of the novel in a few murmured asides, provides a portrait of Duranty in which problems of personality combine with the difficulties he encountered as a writer. One has the feeling that though he was born to be a writer, Duranty was not convinced of the fact, and that he also had doubts about the form he had chosen, finding as many sources of difficulty in art as he did in life, which was in fact only natural, since his purpose was to make art an exact replica of life. There is something constrained and miserable about his temperament, and it is reflected in his fate. He had too many doubts about himself not to inspire the same doubts in the mind of posterity.

A novel such as *The Misfortune of Henriette Gérard* has charm and a scrupulous, naïve perfection that made it certainly one the works most deserving of being read and reread in that second half of the nineteenth century. But the qualities that we see in it today would appear to be rather different from the ones that Duranty thought he was giving to his novel, and perhaps even quite remote from the character which was really that of the book when it first appeared. For its realism is no longer evident to us at all. It is clear that the novelist has broken with Romantic grandiloquence, that he is wary of the oratorical style, aims to paint things as they appear to him and tells a story that was perhaps originally a true one. It is also clear that he is interested in scenes of provincial or rural life, whose character he sometimes emphasizes with the occasional remark. Finally, there are several scenes that show the bourgeoisie in its true light, as a wretched class for which selfishness is traditional and money-mindedness a virtue. But all these features are so lightly drawn that it is easy to see in them not so much an innovation as a reminiscence, so that the ultimate impression we are left with is one of refined and candid literature.

The only feature that still reveals some dependency on a particular genre is the painstaking nature of some of the descriptions, the slow development of the analyses and the sprawling nature of the dialogues, from which not a single response is omitted. To appear true to life, the novelist who cannot say everything will at least want to give the impression that he would like to do so; if he records a large number of insignificant features, it will be tempting to believe that he has done it so as to conform to reality, where the diversity of events makes almost all of them appear unnecessary compared to one or two of them that can be arbitrarily singled out. Unfortunately, however much a writer like Duranty, with his sense of what a literary work should be, has recourse to details whose precision is in inverse proportion to their importance, he brings them so honestly into the story and organizes them according to such skillfully constructed perspectives, that what is insignificant ends up acquiring meaning, and these long developments seem to be justified not by the imitation of reality but by the ordered structure of a well-told tale. All that remains is a naïve, precious, and vain desire to introduce into the novel more facts than it requires, and to induce in the reader a state of attention without focus.

The Misfortune of Henriette Gérard and *Fine William's Cause* resemble psychological novels that are partly unaware that such is what they are, and that derive from this ignorance an authenticity that a profounder level of analysis would have been quite incapable of providing. We read them without knowing—or caring—whether we are dealing with a story, a character portrayal, or a scene from daily life, and this ambiguity, which is in no way calculated, is pleasing for the sort of lulling movement in which it envelops the mind. After all, it

is a pleasure to feel that one has a choice between several subjects of interest, and that if there is one that is missing, if all are
rather slight, together they amount to a fairly robust guarantee
against boredom. What remains, however, is a discreet, harmonious, rather sad little drama of the will. Emile Germain
in *Henriette Gérard* and Louis Leforgeur in *Fine William* are
weak individuals, ill at ease in life, sensitive to ridicule and ill
equipped to be assertive, who are suddenly thrown by the
whim of passion into a difficult situation from which only a
firm and single-minded decision on their part will allow them
to emerge with their happiness intact. But the thought of all
the obstacles involved makes them hesitate. If they act, it is
inopportunely. If they display courage, it is when their courage is of no use to them. They agonize and come to grief, and
finally conclude that it is no easy thing to act. In *The Misfortune of Henriette Gérard* this drama of the will becomes a dual
one. While Emile Germain, who loves Henriette, has not even
managed to ask for her hand in marriage, and is considered
by the richer family he wishes to join as a money-grubbing
seducer, Henriette, who loves Emile, refuses to marry anyone
else, least of all the old man she is presented with, and she
displays a stubborn willfulness that is both ingeniously resis-
tant and firm of purpose. The outcome is that Henriette mar-
ries the man she rejected, because she is attached to the reality
of the world against which she struggles; she is sensitive to its
appeal, and has a vague sense that she will find reasons to be
happy in a marriage that may conflict with her will today, but
that provides her for tomorrow with considerable means for
exercising it. Too much will on one side, too little on the other
leave little hope for mutual happiness.

These stories are perhaps somewhat naïve, but they are so
to the extent that one suspects them of being quite similar to
a real experience that the author has concealed beneath the
conventional plotlines. This sort of psychological autobiogra-
phy, which gives itself an alibi in dramas that are perhaps realist, but exceptional nonetheless, and which ultimately uses

realism as a means of demure confession; these melancholy, meticulous portraits that Duranty provides of himself by making them into masks for empty shadows, all harmoniously divide his stories between truth and convention. All is not false in a work whose author constantly encounters failure and disgrace; and fortunately everything is not real there either, for in order to cloak what is too immediate about the sincerity that motivates him, he requires a novel form that resembles an undisguised simulation. If there is any romanticism about Duranty, or at least a certain ambiguity in his art, it comes from the presumption on his part that he was interested in the real for its own sake, whereas he was only interested in it when his own existence was at stake. He was cheating slightly by proposing to portray a world in which he did not figure, since his sole wish was to portray himself. He the supremely honest writer demonstrated that realism is only ever based on fraud.

The form chosen by Duranty provides another mishap for this writer who rarely did what he wanted to. It is precise, neat, and has few images, but its cadences conform to language and obey its laws. There can be no denying that it gives an impression of style. Duranty, who reproached Flaubert for the demanding nature of his language, wrote novels whose style is their surest quality, and that give the impression of having survived only because they were faithful to what they should have been deprived of, if the theories were to be believed. Thanks to their tone, which reintroduces into the novel genre an eighteenth-century dryness, and thanks also to a particular gift of innocence that makes his observations appear pleasantly simple and pure, his books convey a crystalline impression, the feeling of another world, similar to the melancholy that things would inspire if they were all in a museum, and reduced to being nothing but a touching imitation of themselves, preserved under glass. It should not be forgotten that Duranty ended up writing little puppet plays, and in this miniaturized humanity we can see a symbol for his own books, which still sound such a charming note by endowing characters who are part-real and part-conventional with the delightful voice of a memory.

In short, poor Duranty miscalculates time and again. Having decided to invent realism, he sinks into obscurity while realism goes on to dominate an entire field of literature. Eager to leave an objective portrayal of the world, he succeeds only in leaving a portrait of the portrayer. Convinced that the novel should copy the real by denying itself any literary artifice, he writes works that appeal for their novelistic charm, their antiquated air, and their pleasant style. Finally, but this is his reward, he wished like every good realist to be read by everyone, whereas he is prized by those rarest of minds who cherish what is rare: Baudelaire, André Suarès, Jean Paulhan.

—June 29, 1942

Realism's Chances

Hard on the heels of Marc Bernard, Louis Guilloux has just written a novel about an impoverished childhood. His young hero lives the humblest of lives. His home is a former stable where light scarcely penetrates, and whose paltry furnishings turn it into a hovel. This ramshackle place looks onto a yard where a disreputable café denies the neighborhood any semblance of respectability, and permanently cuts those who live there off from the world of decent folk. "Rue du Tonneau lowlife" is what they are. The streets without pavements, the windowless houses and the dirty shops are merely picturesque ruins that are doomed to be demolished. One day the wreckers will make off with the debris. Where will the inhabitants find refuge then? They live in fear of having to relinquish their poverty. Something worse than poverty awaits them.

Like *Just Like Children*, *Bread of Dreams* portrays the grace, innocence, and vision of childhood in colors that would normally eclipse it yet do not spoil its purity.[1] The means Louis Guilloux employs are very different from those of Marc Bernard. He is without sobriety; his descriptions need to be ponderous in order to leave a trace in the mind; he requires details that accumulate in a sort of controlled expansion, forming a dense narrative that is closed in on every side and powerfully built out of stone. In the course of these developments, which are solid rather than flimsy, we discover the most delicate of minds, sentiment at its most refined and an intention of the heart that captures things in their brilliance and their gentleness. It is a robust art that is vibrant with artistic subtlety. It draws from itself more than its technique seemed to promise.

This novel, which received the Populist Literature prize, is in no way constrained by its genre, and even less by any sort of partisan outlook. Its characters are of course the most modest of people, its plot is provided by the slow unfolding of an unhappy youth, and dust, grime, and poverty coat its realism with a dull layer through which the images of hope become less and less visible. But this world of penury is not a world of unhappiness. On the contrary, we are constantly drawn to a light that is like the truth of objects; it is as if human encounter, however unjust the human condition may be, is enough to keep alive all the prospects for joy, dreams, and freedom from care with which the community of men enriches its inner life. When the author tells of the bedbugs and lice that disturb the sleep of his little heroes and against which they struggle to no avail; or when he evokes the words of an inconsiderate schoolteacher who punishes the poorest children as a penalty for their poverty, what emanates from these wordless scenes is a sense of tranquil humanity, authentic truth, and natural simplicity, opening up a store of dignity and nobility that nothing can threaten.

The two parts of *Bread of Dreams* are not of equal interest. The second, which develops around the eccentricities of a seductive, energetic, and amoral female cousin, is picturesque rather than engaging, and the story evaporates in a succession of episodes that teach us nothing concerning the people about whom we would like to know everything. But the first part is much more successful. The central character is the grandfather. In the stable that has been converted into a humble dwelling, an old man who is racked by terrible fits of coughing and who spends his entire day mending clothes, works at a table by the window. He has inexplicable bouts of anger and incomprehensible habits. He is kindhearted, secretive, and rustic. Though not religious, he has a liking for the pomp of religious ceremonies, and takes part in the Procession of the plague-stricken. He discreetly listens to concerts. He is ground down by poverty and endures his life with patience. He is a solitary who is perhaps unaware of his solitude, but who lives at the furthest possible remove from things and men. He remains a mystery, as would any man whose authority children have a sense of, and whom they love without knowing why.

There are no extraordinary episodes in this long story. But at the same time, everything gives the impression that the extraordinary can be found in the humdrum life of the simple folk we encounter every day. The imagination and sensibility of children have no need to reject daily life in order to find the gaiety they cannot do without. And this gaiety, which is sometimes painful or dramatic, adds no false color to the feeling that comes naturally from things. The child sees what is and, without transforming it, extracts its truth, which is made up of harmony, purity, and precision. There is nothing imaginary about his vision, but the movements of lightness and ease that characterize him, his indifference to the laws of gravity, the way he goes from a walk to a jump, from a run back to the stroll which is his regular pace, make him a truthful witness who is never crushed by the truth, and who can judge all ponderous human detail with the requisite degree of childishness. Louis Guilloux's art, like that of Marc Bernard, suggests that realism escapes its limits when it reproduces the pattern of our earliest memories. Realism is thus perhaps justifiable to the extent that it is the expression of innocence, which is itself, according to Jean Giraudoux's definition, simply the perfect adaptation of a being to the universe in which he lives. An innocent is someone who offers no explanation, for whom life is both mysterious and totally clear, and who is without recrimination. And in the same way, realism presupposes a feeling of complete equality, of absolute fellowship and sympathy with all beings, all races and all species, both moral and physical—a feeling that is probably possible only in childhood.

Canisy by Jean Follain is not a story of childhood, but it evokes a village where a child once lived, and it employs exactness and precision in the same way that *Bread of Dreams* does, in order to express a child's view of things.[2] In the space of a hundred pages, without ever making an error or putting a foot wrong, Jean Follain goes from the level of appearances, where superficial description seems an adequate portrayal, to that level of reality which generally escapes the eye and reveals itself only to an exacting poetic instinct. The Surrealists familiarized us with this discovery of the object. In a poet like Paul Éluard, there is an extraordinary coincidence between the words he seems to reinvent and the things he seems to rediscover. In a painter such as Pierre Roy, there is a wish to capture the object as it is, in its absolute truth, and to enshrine it, decked out in its objective glory, at the center of a world that henceforth exists only to extol it. Jean Follain, who as a poet passed momentarily through the Surrealist flame, has also retained from this brief station a sense of the mystery of the object and a belief that this mystery is perfectly rendered by the appearances that describe it.

His little book would seem to be one of the best he has published. Without the aid of a story, in precisely balanced scenes, he gradually brings to light the different aspects of a village just like any other, yet that, the more it becomes indistinguishable from the memories that each person thinks they discover within them, becomes more and more singular, and so to speak the archetype of every existing village. Jean Follain evokes figures that represent only themselves, and whom it seems possible to see only once: his maternal grandmother Heussebrot, his paternal grandfather the schoolmaster,

Florentine the servant girl, or Paul the village idiot. But these simple characters, who appear inseparable from one person's memory, are endowed by the enigma of their simplicity with an emblematic character, and quietly take the place of those images that are the birthright of every childhood. Furthermore this village, which is so scrupulously described, whose geographical location, whose hamlets, roads, bridge, and river become familiar to us, appears as a focus of poetic forces, a receptacle for all the things to which a poet's eye can become attached in the course his life. Occasionally, a writer brings to life a town in which the figures of his invention or the adventures of which he dreams are constantly reappearing; Jouhandeau's Chaminadour is an example of this. But in evoking Canisy, Follain seems to do no more than describe the place where all the beings he creates really exist, and to which he turns each time he needs to discover fantastic, unimaginable objects such as "a darning-egg made of yellow varnished boxwood for mending stockings, a flat iron shaped like a heart, a horse brass, a star, a helmet-plume holder . . ."

Every scene from *Canisy* is composed with the intention of extracting from the juxtaposition of two simple images—indeed, the simplest images possible—a complex sentiment that will stave off oblivion. The details are chosen less for what they are, than for what they become when placed alongside others which set them vibrating. For example, when Follain speaks of the servant girl's mother, he writes: "I have a very distant image of old Mrs. Simon, the mother of Florentine my maternal grandmother's servant. I gave her the almost Asian name Ma Yo-Yo. Dressed in rough gray clothes and wearing a white cotton bonnet, on entering the hall with its mosaic floor she was always careful not to make a noise with her clogs." Immediately afterward, he adds this other detail: "I saw her grave when it was still fresh, and no grass had yet sprung up between the clumps of earth." Similarly, language resorts to the simplest words, which, because they are used sparingly, tend to stand out through unexpected juxtapositions. This is not strictly speaking a matter of surprise effects, but rather of a development in which the way the words follow on from each other is more important than their choice. Hence Follain writes: "She was born in 1830, in an era when sounds were so precise in a village without machines, and when there was still the sorcerer's house, its clay baking in the sun, while he, in his doorway, kept watch, dressed in a lordly flowered waistcoat." The image of the village without machines, then that of the sorcerer's house exposed to the sun, and then of the sorcerer himself, portrayed with an attitude and a costume that are equally expressive, are all innocently associated with each other as if they were naturally linked, whereas they form a fragile chain which seems to reproduce the idiosyncrasy of memory. Perhaps tricks like these would require a surer, purer language. But there is real purity both in the composition of the work and in its imagery, which can be modest or humble, but never servile.

If these two books about childhood bear the stamp of realism, which is to say, of a wish to express reality by creating the illusion that it can be expressed directly, without any literary intermediary, on the contrary *Invitation to Life* by Jacques Robert, which is a novel of adolescence, has recourse to impressionism, which is a refusal to look at what is without involving movements of the soul, reactions of sensibility, and everything that requires the particular logic of metaphor in order to become visible.[3] It is perhaps perfectly normal that what is opinionated about youth, its fragmentary vision, its outlandish, unstable emotions, should require an art of discontinuity in which localized notation and acutely unique instants can be expressed. In this respect, Jean Giraudoux's first books, *School for the Indifferent*, *Simon the Pathetic*, and *Suzanne and the Pacific*, displayed the perfection with which his dialectical art of the image corresponded to the moods, dreams, and fantasies of youth. Jacques Robert's novel is partly written under the influence of the same stars. And several pages shine with the brilliance of precious stones and crystal, of gold or silver coins, which, to use Albert Thibaudet's expression, are coin of the realm among the great Symbolist writers. But Jacques Robert was not content with such hyperbole. He has introduced into the pure world of words and figures the fait accompli of analysis, and the ponderousness of often realistic dialogue. His book becomes unbelievable as a result. It is implausible in so far as it has recourse to the usual ingredients of truth, presenting its five young people as they discover friendship as real figures, and describing their adventures, their search for a life in common, and the failure of this community of friends, after the fashion of a novelist who claims to tell of what he has seen. The use of images ceases to be a means of creation and becomes merely a descriptive process. Jacques Robert's art is rich in talent, but he squanders it by creating a mixture in which optical illusion seeks in vain to connect with forms that belong to the inner world.

—July 1, 1942

Jupiter, Mars, Quirinus

If Georges Dumézil's book *Jupiter, Mars, Quirinus* were of interest only to the specialist, it would be deprived of part of the readership it deserves and to which it appeals thanks to the brilliance if its form, the scope of its attention to certain specific issues and the skill with which it draws the reader toward questions whose legitimacy can be glimpsed only at the highest levels of learning.[1] The latest in a series of numerous studies in comparative mythology, his essay not only examines problems relating to the prehistoric past of our civilizations, it also presupposes a method that requires us to reflect usefully on what the requirements of knowledge are, and it helps to define a notion as important and as obscure as that of myth.

We shall confine ourselves to summarizing briefly one or two of Dumézil's views. It has seemed for a long time that little that was valid could ever be known about the unified civilization constituted by India and Asia—the Indo-Europeans— before they were dispersed throughout Europe. During the nineteenth century, after the discovery of a common language to which Sanskrit, Greek, Latin, and the Germanic, Celtic, Slavonic, and Baltic languages were related, comparativists believed they could reconstitute the religion and the mythology of these remote societies. The attempt was premature, and it failed. But for the last twenty years or so new research, developments in ethnography and anthropology and an increasing mistrust of sociological theories have made it possible to reconsider that failure, and Dumézil's studies are themselves an example of the combination of rigor and daring that has been necessary in order to formulate some initial hypotheses concerning the religious and social frameworks of the Indo-Europeans.

It could well have been the case that no surviving relic provided proof of the unity of this ancient civilization. But between Indo-European society and the historic peoples who descended from it, and who are so remote from it that what they inherit from it appears imperceptible, intermediary formations were available for examination and allowed comparisons to be made. In the Far East, for example, an Indo-Iranian formation can be observed; and in the Far West, one that links the peoples destined to become the Celts and the Italiots. These systems, which are already much closer to the Indo-European synchrony, make it easier to grasp the presumed features of their common origin thanks to the resemblances they sometimes retain. Moreover, it is a fact that quite a few words with a common root and which concern religion appear both among the Italiots and the Celts as well as in the Indo-Iranian group, and appear only there. That is a sign that in these intermediary civilizations, beneath the renewed forms of myth and ritual, common usages and related religious forms had survived, and these forms and usages may be regarded as the legacy of early Indo-European society.

Dumézil devotes his main effort to comparing a number of elements from the Far East and the Far West, and particularly to the analogy that can be observed between the triple hierarchy of Brahminic society (priests, warriors, herders/farmers) and the triple hierarchy of the most august of the Roman priesthoods (flamens of Jupiter, Mars, and Quirinus), with all the religious, social, and political notions that are associated with each of them. The division of Indo-Iranian society into three precisely differentiated and hierarchical casts is well known, and it is equally certain that the Indo-Iranians based their ideal structure, the order of their world and that of their gods, on this harmonious threefold model. In ancient Rome, Dumézil finds significant traces of a similar classification. The three major flamens dedicated to the archaic triad represent a religious configuration in which Jupiter is associated with the sacred, Mars with warfare, and Quirinus with fertility and abundance. Several signs indicate moreover that this hierarchy of function (magic, war, fertility), which is similar to that which inspired the Indo-Iranian casts, corresponded to a certain view of the world, and illustrated a division of society into three clans: priests, magicians, and lawyers; military nobility; and herders/farmers.

The three early Roman tribes, whose strange names—the Ramnes, the Lucernes, the Tities and Tatians—intrigue the ancients themselves, seem to represent in the Roman mind the echo of a tradition corresponding to a functional distribution of society that is given added complexity by a contractual merger between peoples. The Ramnes are associated with a notion of the priority of politics combined with religious activity; the Lucernes (named after Lucerno, an Etruscan warrior who came to the aid of Romulus against the Sabines) with the notion of warlike technique; and the Tities, who represented the Sabines, with all of the agrarian cults and modes of worship. Dumézil provides a new interpretation of the Sabine War, whose mythical significance is established in his view by the way it corresponds to the Germanic legend of the Vanes and the Ases. Like the Vanes and the Ases, the Sabines and the Romans are neighboring nations, and nations that each have their specialism, since Freyr the god of the Vanes and Tatius the Sabine king will later fulfill for their former adversaries the function of fertility and abundance which each of them represents. Like the war of the Ases and the Vanes, that between the Romans and the Sabines is only of interest for the treaty that puts an end to it. In both cases, the effect of that treaty is to introduce into a community where the sovereign religious function and the warrior function are already embodied, the principal members or all of the representatives of the third function. The mechanisms coincide in every detail. As a result, it is possible to see in this war not so much a simple historical event as a myth destined to reveal what exchanges led to the establishment of normal relations between the original functional classes, that is to say between religious Sovereignty and warlike Force on one hand and Fertility on the other. The fact that the Romans provide a local and historical representation of this phenomenon can be explained, according to Dumézil, by their particular attitude toward the universe; whereas in India and Scandinavia what emerged was a myth, in Rome this was replaced by a tale of war, a story with dates linked to a historically defined individual; the monster or demon becomes an adversary whom annalists believe they can identify; Romulus and Numa, who are both simply kings in whom creative, magical power and the lawmaking mentality are combined, are the equivalents of the magician-god Varuna and the god Mithra. Roman mythology needs to be true to life and historical. It is the "past" of Rome itself, and this past has the same meaning as marvelous fables of the other world have for other peoples.

It is not possible in this brief summary to follow Dumézil as far as the various conclusions that his analyses make possible. He takes it as a given that the Indo-Europeans saw the world and society as made up of three hierarchical organisms providing three functions: magic and legal administration, warlike force, and fertility. So copious are the traces of these configurations on Roman soil that they seem to have corresponded over a long period to a system that remained vigorous. Only in the Etruscan period do the changes become decisive, when Rome grants the city a preeminence that transforms its entire outlook on the world, and in particular the memories of its distant past. The oldest traditions of the Dorians and the Ionians also bear the traces of a society divided into classes (priests, warriors, third estate); and Dumézil cannot resist seeing in Plato's ideal city, harmoniously constructed around philosophers who govern, warriors who fight, and plowmen and artisans who produce, a reminder of Indo-European forms. What is striking, all told, is that Hindu myths and thinkers, like the Druids, should seek to discern within souls the same architectural and hierarchical order that exists in kingdoms, in accordance with a notion of which Plato provides a celebrated account in Book IV of the *Republic*. Is this homology between the soul and society an Indo-European legacy? Is it not present too in the traditions that the vestiges of non-Aryan civilizations allow us to imagine? It is in this respect that the comparative method appears threatened by the range of its hypotheses and the scale of its success, claiming more than it is able to and more than can possibly be proved.

It must be remarked, however, that such a method, however extraordinary it may seem when set against the usual demands of scientific knowledge, is vital to the development of comparative philology. That discipline always presupposes a little more than is allowed by the other disciplines of which it is the synthesis. It would seem that as long as it exists only as a two-way movement between the specialist fields of philology and mythology, as a method of research and interpretation carried out using evidence already obtained by specialists in each language, it ought only to begin its task once the development of those specific disciplines is complete. Such is not the case. In advance of analyzing the terms that it is its purpose to bring into relation with each other, the comparative method in matters of religion and language often establishes hypotheses. It claims to grasp as a whole what is not yet fully graspable in its particulars. Dumézil alludes to the accusations of imprudence leveled by specialist philologists at a method that owes everything to them, and yet makes use of its inheritance before the latter has even been fully constituted. No doubt this accusation is sometimes justified. But the comparativist's aim is important to the extent that it reminds us of the illusions of analysis. The world does not allow itself to be broken down into parts in such a way that the painstaking, methodical study of the parts can provide knowledge of the world. The method that permits the search for the elements is itself a hypothesis concerning the whole. The science of human realities is only possible if there is an awareness of this anticipatory factor, this movement beyond the facts, and if the methodical rigor and discipline for which proof is the reward are applied to a moment of knowledge in which proof is suspended.

Frequently opposed to specialized knowledge, the comparative method does not always accord with historical knowledge. The image Dumézil provides of early Rome, the interpretations of the story of Rome's foundation that he offers are of a sort that is likely to elicit from historians a number of objections, which he anticipates and whose legitimacy he does not contest. A historian will always have difficulty accepting that the relations between the Romans and the Sabines, the war that divided them and the treaty that reunited them, can be entirely explained as fictions and do not leave behind a residue consisting simply of facts and events. For a mythologist, stories of the origins of Rome are legends that justify or express the structure of the early people; perhaps they also correspond to real events (Dumézil acknowledges that Rome certainly incorporated Sabines and Etruscans), but they can be entirely accounted for if they are seen as a set of fictional details underlying customs, cults, and features of political or religious organization. If historical fact survives, it appears as devoid of justification; it is superfluous. What is real in the stories is not the series of events that these stories provide; it is the system of concepts, the nature of the social and religious forms that they translate into marvelous or realistic episodes. The war between the Sabines and the Romans is no more or less legendary than the war between the gods of the Ases and the gods of the Vanes for the Germans, since in both cases these are stories designed to express, in different guises, the harmonious relations within a given society between the higher classes (priests and warriors) and the rural class.

The main characteristic of myths as authors such as Dumézil understand them is thus never to be disinterested, nor to correspond in any way to the free inventions of the imagination. They are necessarily related to customs, observances, and rituals whose repercussions within the general awareness they convey. They are never without significance and rarely without purpose; or at least, there has always been a moment in the time-scale of a myth when it has served to explain, reveal or maintain a form of social life. In that sense there is nothing more real than a myth, nothing truer than a fable. And legend appears as an illustration of that strange inability of the collective mind to lose itself in pure fictions and forge vain lies.

—July 8, 1942

In the Land of Magic

It is perhaps natural that when art enters into a union with enigma and withdraws from ordinary forms, it should lose the advantages afforded by easy success. There is nothing more dismal than the vulgarization of monsters, which places within reach of everyone what is strange, that is to say what must always remain foreign to us. One of the weaknesses of Surrealism lay in its susceptibility to success. The mass of people were invited so to speak into a forbidden universe, where they could live on familiar terms with horrible species whose significance is precisely that they must remain hidden, and exclude all possibility of a familiar life. The fact that the Surrealists aspired to be as it were directors of souls, and were always attracted by action without perceiving its constraints, goes some way to explaining a decline in which people are rather too ready today to include any profound and authentic movement.

By its very nature, the art of Henri Michaux has remained remote, in our view, from the naïve glory that the extraordinary and the unusual complacently court, as if the extraordinary could become the rule and the unusual become customary. His influence has grown from year to year, without being linked in any way to a search for ways of manipulating minds and using surprise to obtain their admiration. A talk by André Gide, which was known about initially for having failed to take place, gave an account of works such as *Ecuador, A Barbarian in Asia*, and *Journey to Great Garabagne*, which served more to gratify those who already knew Henri Michaux than to make too available to the public a beauty which still remained hidden. And indeed, this poet writes very little, or rather leads us to believe that the little he does write provides the measure of his own peculiar inventiveness, as if for some authors there were no better sign of abundance than their ability to limit the use they make of practical resources with which they are richly endowed.

A slim volume published some time ago under the title *In the Land of Magic*, and an exhibition of drawings and watercolors that has just taken place in a gallery in Saint-Germain-des Prés, convey most effectively the utter purity of the enigmas that Michaux produces.[1] The monsters he brings to life, the baroque forms that his pen calls forth, and the fantastic practices he describes have as their principal feature the fact that they do not correspond to some mysterious significance, and are entirely what they appear. Whereas the fantastic for Swift is a path toward a social myth, and whereas the extraordinary for Edgar Allan Poe is the momentary appearance of an elusive substantial world, both Henri Michaux's figures and his stories exclude interpretation, presuppose nothing except what they show, and draw their entire meaning from the way they make the mind wish to go no further. Such a privilege has its value. It is a remarkable thing to endow mystery with a sort of self-evidence, to make the mysterious not what cannot be seen but what is manifest, to make what must always remain absent and what is present with no justification other than its presence coincide by means of a curious mirror-effect. Mystery's way of being, for Henri Michaux, is to assert itself absolutely with neither outcome nor end, to be entirely there with no possibility that its existence might be augmented by some explanation or other. You understand what is strange only when it refuses to be compared with anything else (even though it is only real in relation to something other), and transforms you into itself.

The brief tableaux that make up *In the Land of Magic* are as natural as any description of the ordinary world—indeed, much more natural. The question is not whether these images correspond to some possible reality or are true to life through their internal harmony and inner order. It is their spontaneity and their lack of purpose that make them fascinating, by replacing the mind that founds everything on unity with a deeper mind that is free from that demonstrative coherence. "On a main road," Michaux says in one of his short stories, "it is not uncommon to see a wave, a solitary wave, a wave separated from the ocean. It is of no use, and is not an occasion for play. It is a case of magical spontaneity." This magic, whose tricks he devotes himself to recounting from the point of view of someone who does not understand them, in a scarcely imaginary land, is none other than his art itself, which is dedicated to preventing what in fact should be considered devoid of sense from appearing senseless.

Who are these Magi whose powers cannot be said to be either real or not real? Everyone, or almost everyone. There comes a moment in the exercise of their knowledge when fiction is produced as spontaneously as speech. Healers heal themselves without meaning to. "Bleeding on the wall, alive, red or partly infected, is the wound of a man; of a Magus who has put it there. Why? Out of asceticism, the better to suffer from it; because were it on his person, he would not be able to refrain from healing it, using his thaumaturgical powers, which come so naturally to him that he is completely unconscious of them. But in this fashion, he keeps it for a long time, without it closing up. This process is common." Others, "though they know perfectly well that the stars are something besides huge lights on the surface of the sky, cannot resist making pretend stars to delight their children, to delight themselves, rather as an exercise, out of magical spontaneity." Sometimes it is as if magic is merely the dizzy attraction of what does not exist for beings who can respond to only the imaginary. "What is most interesting about the country cannot be seen. You can be sure that you have not seen it. . . . Hence the Federal Capital remained inaccessible and invisible to me, even though I was told goodness knows how many times how to get there, and definitely spent a week almost touching it." The guilty man, placed in the center of empty arenas, is confounded by the silence that to him seems like a deafening interrogation. From cupboards and cellars, from everywhere that is dark, come ghostly images that then vanish, a bloodied head, a hanged man, a toad, objects from a phantasmagoria that are merely a furtive imitation of real things. But this distinction between reality and appearance is bound to fail in a world where what imitates life is indistinguishable from life itself. What does the executioner do? By sheer force of will, he rips off the face of felons caught in the act. The operation is described as if it were real. "If the operation is skillfully executed, the whole face comes away, forehead, eyes, cheeks, the entire front part of the head, as if it had been wiped off with some sort of corrosive sponge."

But at the same time, through a single detail ("It requires incredible willpower to detach a face, accustomed as it is to its man"), Henri Michaux implies also that it is all just a horrible estrangement—the executioner turning the face that is the inseparable expression of a man into something unusual, external to itself—so that the description, in spite of its precision and sobriety, becomes as ambiguous as if it were preserved the way a nightmare is by the vagueness of night.

The form best suited to giving style to these dreams is as simple, even as commonplace, as can be. The reader must not feel mystified by the words. He needs to be led toward the extraordinary by a tone that is least likely to make him believe something extraordinary. He must find himself on an equal footing with the unsayable thanks to words drawn from every-day usage. One of Michaux's rare gifts is a sort of humor, which consists in taking language at its basest level in order to make it express beings and objects that correspond to fabulous metaphoric inventions. And yet there is nothing more expressive than the choice of these lackluster words: If someone turns up when a death is announced, and blackens and darkens everything with magical stains and ash, he is "the mourning-spreader"; in every block of stone there is a fragment that must be discovered so it can be handled effortlessly; it is "the marble tooth." "The Water Shepherd whistles up a spring and hey presto! here it comes, emerging from its bed and following behind him." "What would I do with the gift of the Bow?" asks a Magus. All these words are, as it were, reformed by a usage that adapts them to new relations and invests them with a poetic charge to which sensibility absent-mindedly yields.

One of the scenes from *In the Land of Magic* describes the Canapas tree: "The Canapas tree probably produces spittle in order to express its feelings, for it is during the hottest part of the day, when the trumpets pass, when a fanfare can be heard, that at the base of its largest branches a strange brown secretion appears in irregular bursts. Is this suffering? Is it joy? With an embarrassed feeling you observe this surge, which slows as the musicians head off into the distance, before disappearing along with them, as the tree once again becomes as tightly closed as a casket." This type of fantastic writing is very close to the methodical observation with which Francis Ponge creates very precise effects in a little book in the "Metamorphoses" collection entitled *The Voice of Things*.[2] Here also we find brief descriptions of rain, autumn's end, the orange, the loaf of bread, or the pebble—nature studies, so to speak—that share with those of Jules Renard a taste for the picturesque and the ingenious remark. When Francis Ponge says the following about snails, he is merely giving an image a mischievous meaning, which clarifies the description without going any deeper:

"Surely it must sometimes be a burden to have to carry this shell everywhere they go, but they don't complain and in the long run they are quite happy to do so. It's a boon to be able to retreat indoors wherever you may be, and keep your distance from people who are a nuisance." But these mannerisms by no means exhaust the significance of analyses in which things reveal their veritable structure in the very process of being described. What is a tree? You can endow it with a divine nature, like Ronsard, or strange customs, like Henri Michaux. Francis Ponge is content with totally rigorous observations that gradually reveal its way of being. The tree is immobile; it does not have a voice; it does not make any movements; it expresses itself only in poses; once and for all it says what it is; however many leaves or branches it puts out, it merely repeats thousands of times that it is a tree; it is inseparable from the trace it inscribes and through which, as it develops in space, it analyzes itself indefinitely. What is water? Liquid is what refuses all shape by definition and yields to its own weight; the urge to fall which is peculiar to it to such a degree, allowing it constantly to escape and at the same time making it depend entirely on what collects it, transforms it into a sort of manic reality, obsessed with a single urge, its *idée fixe*, which is to descend ever lower, humiliating itself in a fall that can never satisfy it.

It is clear that Francis Ponge endows objects not with feelings or intentions drawn from their vague likeness to men, but with a way of being that is their rule, and in accordance with which every piece of exact description is undertaken. Something cannot be described unless you have discovered its bent, its *parti pris*, the obedience to itself that allows it to endure through every metamorphosis. It is style that, in the dense tangle of appearances, recasts forms in accordance with the law it finds in them, and it is through style that Francis Ponge uncovers the truth of these objects. His own style is that of an excellent writer. It is lively, swift, and sure of its movements and its images; it is sometimes capable of transmutation, but it is also quizzical, precise, and disdainful. The value of these poetic sketches can be judged if we recreate the world of presentiment, analysis, and verbal study that the following simple reverie on the subject of autumn presupposes, in a page where abstract fantasy is admirably combined with a sense of the beautiful:

> Tired of holding back all winter, trees are suddenly persuaded that they've been had. They cannot keep it up any longer: they let fly with their words in a flood, a vomit of green. They attempt to come entirely into leaf as words. Too bad! It will all sort itself out as best it can! As a matter of fact, it does sort itself out! There is no freedom at all in foliation. . . . They put out twigs on which to hang yet more words: our trunks are there, they think to themselves, to take on everything. They do their best to hide, to blend in with each other. Believing they can say everything, and blanket the whole world with a full range of words: all they say is "trees." They are even incapable of detaining the birds, which fly off again just as they were rejoicing at having produced such curious flowers. Ever the same leaf, ever the same way of unfolding, and the same edge, always leaves that are symmetrical with themselves, hanging symmetrically! Try one more leaf!—Same thing! Yet another! Same thing! Ultimately, nothing can stop them except suddenly this remark: "You don't get away from trees by using trees." A new weariness ensues, and a new change of mood. "Let all that turn yellow and fall. Bring on the taciturn state, the denuding, autumn."

—July 15, 1942

Ghost Story

Franz Hellens is a Belgian writer who fully deserves our attention and esteem, and one of the few living writers to have devoted his talents as a novelist to portraying the fantastic side of the world, using either classical or traditional forms. For more than twenty years he has published tales that are the direct descendants of the admirable writing that was once widespread in America, England, and Romantic Germany, and whose influence on French writers was and remains considerable. His latest book, *New Fantastic Realities*, is made up of stories in which genuine ghosts sometimes appear, and where a number of strange freaks of nature are skillfully described.[1] It will be read with the sort of pleasure that is generally associated with startling and even horrible visions.

These brief notes are not really the place in which to reconsider the role played in modern art by the search for what Goethe and German Romanticism called the "nocturnal side" of the soul. Everyone can recall those works that have traversed our times and that, even when they fall outside the ambit of our admiration, retain the power to act upon us like dark, invisible stars that are extinct and yet still remain capable of falling anew. But it must be observed that this desire to seize hold of man in the dizzying succession of his slips and his stumblings [*faux pas*], this enquiry which has led art to replace a world of clarity with a world without perspective or color, this passion for what can be neither seen nor known, has been accompanied by a disdain for the literary work as such; and having pulverized the day and its light, it has gone further and sought to reduce to dust the balance and the form of the fiction that was destined to receive the debris of visible nature. Was such a consequence necessary? Was it inevitable that the portrayal of a flattened world, exposed to the workings of a blind, unknowable Fate, should cause the work in which that portrayal was meant to take place to crumble? Such questions merit too lengthy an enquiry for us to linger over them now, but one thing at least is certain, as André Malraux has rightly observed: What separates William Faulkner from Edgar Allan Poe or Hoffmann is not an obsession with nocturnal forces, or a terrorized craving for the shadows that embody the absurd, or even the nature of the visions that represent these values; it is a concern for the work of art, for the story, which in the case of the author of the *Tales of Mystery and Imagination* is close to acquiring an objective existence that is perfect and complete, whereas the novelist of *As I Lay Dying* refuses to submit to its demands (though only partially it should be said).

It is in this sense that Franz Hellens stands aloof from turbulent modernity and gives the impression of being a classical author. His tales are governed by a story that must inevitably be told. The entire mystery or secret whose presence he seeks to represent is expressed in a story, that is to say a series of episodes, the main justification for whose development lies in the simple fact that they form a series. There is a serious difference in a novel or a tale between story and plot. E. M. Forster, who some time ago devoted one of his lecture series in Cambridge to a study of the novel, distinguishes between the two by observing that plot is a narrative in which facts are linked by a relation of cause and effect, whereas story will only allow a pure and simple succession.[2] "The king died, then the queen died" is a story. "The king died, then the queen died of grief" is a plot. He offers another example: "The queen died, and no one knew why until one day it was discovered that the king's death had plunged her into mortal grief." That, says Forster, is the type of plot that involves mystery, which is a form capable of a very high degree of development. And it is a form such as that which fantastic tales often adhere to, at least those written by Hellens. The reader who reads tales of the extraordinary wants to be carried away in a headlong flight during which he repeatedly asks, "And then? And then?" while asking this other question under his breath: "But why? Why?" For him, the tearing pace of the story briefly stands in for verisimilitude. The story is justified because his attention has sped from the beginning to the end without openly requiring any other justification than that repeated "and then?" But this justification is merely provisional. The mystery retains all of its power only because it makes its presence felt for reasons other than the skillful ordering of the narrative, and regardless of whether such narrative adroitness is absolutely authentic and necessary. A cause for it must be found which is not an explanation (for the explanation of a mystery lies solely in the development of its obscurities, it is never a revelation of its secret); it requires a reply which nonetheless does not cause the question to disappear, which rather makes it more pressing, more opaque, more able to turn the mind away from those expressions that guarantee it peace and contentment.

Hellens's tales are sometimes highly effective as stories, but less successful as plots. Those with the greatest allure, such as "The Fog," succeed in totally eliminating the "And why?" or else appeal to traditional beliefs that are there only as innocent conventions. The stranger who settles in Munich and lives with an old landlady receives an advance on our curiosity that is duly honored. Every evening, the old woman comes to see her lodger, driven by the urge to tell him her story, but driven also by another urge whose violence is not immediately apparent. In earlier times she was attached to the Wittelsbach household, and has retained memories of that vanished life that naturally haunt her. She recalls poor Ludwig II, and she thinks she is flattering her guest by remarking that his hair is exactly like the king's. She repeats this remark on successive evenings, and so insistently that the stranger is afraid she will run her hands through his hair. Because she is dirty, old, and rather hideous, though friendly all the same, he finds the idea intolerable, and he succeeds by dint of his discretion in obliging the old woman to maintain an appropriate distance. One evening there is a knock at his door. "Here is my old woman and her cat," he says to himself; but no, it is an old man, the landlady's husband, come to tell him that she passed away that afternoon. The stranger goes back to his work. Toward the end of the evening, he hears a scratching at his door, and in comes the cat, which has been driven to distraction by the death of its mistress. Then he sits back down at his table to work. "A few moments later," he recounts, "behind me, by the door, I heard the soft sound that I knew so well, that of a duster dabbing at the furniture. My hair stood on end with horror. I hadn't the strength to turn round. The dabs with the duster continued, and I heard them progress in the usual direction, by the wardrobe, then the bed, along the bookcase and finally closer to me, ever closer; my brow was covered in a cold sweat; someone placed a hand on my head, ran their fingers, slowly, through my hair."

Clearly, the value of this story is derived very consciously from tradition. A sort of mist that constantly bathes the town simultaneously lulls the gaze and gives objects an existence that is akin to sleep. The reader cannot know if the scene is the effect of a hallucination or not, and indeed he does not wish to know, for it is in the nature of a hallucinatory tale to make any question of objectivity quite fruitless, by showing that errors of the senses are just as replete with tragedy and anguish as any claim to have actually observed some abnormal object. The "why?" thus disappears, or almost does. Conversely, in those tales where Hellens tries to transpose a particular dream-truth into realist fiction, the story often becomes too ponderous; it is like a clumsily assembled machine that cancels out its own function and allows the creativity that set it in motion to go to waste. In the classic versions, terror or a sense of the uncanny is a sort of trap where, once caught, the reader sees with silent horror that he is bogged down in something unspeakable that is much more terrifying than the story itself, and is a sort of indistinct myth. That is true of most American and English tales, be they by Poe, Hawthorne, Fitz James O'Brien, or Stevenson. It is eminently the case with the admirable Achim von Arnim or with Hoffmann. The latter, whose work has in effect been vulgarized owing to the small number of rather cruel tales of his that are always being referred to, had the merit of providing a vision of the extraordinary founded not on fright, but on a pure love of dream. *The Golden Pot* (which Jean Duren has just published in a new translation) and *The Princess Brambilla* open up the humdrum world using a key provided by a dream of happiness that contains almost no disharmony, and is freed of all burdens and all heaviness.[3] We slide from real objects to the treasures of a fabulous existence where sensations, far from disappearing, are richer, more closely knit, and deeper-seated than those of ordinary life. Since sensation is the principle that governs dream, it is also the principle behind an enchantment that creates a supernatural impression out of what is most enduring in nature. It is out of scents, colors, and crystal-clear sounds, that is to say everything that is generally present in our everyday existence, that there arises a feeling of something inextricable by virtue of its intoxication, something incredible by virtue of its unexpectedness. We are astonished by what we know best, enraptured by what we see every day with a jaded eye. And we wake up surrounded by monsters and aerial deities, images that fill each one of our days.

But that enchantment is only possible because the poet's phantasmagorias gravitate around an original experience which gives them an authenticity and a seriousness to which we in our turn are drawn. The myth of the *Golden Pot*, of the blazing lily and the green snake, the adventure of Anselm who succeeds in winning the love of Serpentina through poetry, faith, and dream, by escaping the earthly charms of Veronica, is, rather as with Nerval's *Aurelia*, the transposition of Hoffmann's love for Julia Marc, his young pupil form Bamberg, whom he eventually sacrificed in order to be able to live, poor but free, in total harmony with his art. This Romantic ideal which, seen in its prosaic form, appears distinctly colorless and ineffectual to us today, finds in a work such as *The Golden Pot* a pure and original life once again, a sort of pristine richness. The work prolongs the duration of the "instant" and of the illumination in which it originated, and through a combination of flesh and spirit, a mixture of warmth, intimacy and abstraction, it immortalizes the concrete experience whose absence no skill could possibly compensate for. It is to such privileged instants that one of Hoffmann's heroes refers when he cries, "A special star reigns over me at important moments; into reality it introduces fabulous things which no one believes in and which sometimes appear to me to come from my innermost depths. But then, outside of me, they take on a different value and become the mystical symbols of that dimension of the marvelous that, at every instant of life, lies before our eyes." And such is the "truth" of all fantastic literature.

It is not impossible that one of these "instants" when what is indefinable seems to come to light lies behind Dominique Rolin's recent novel *The Marshes*.[4] But this upsurge of sincerity is overlaid with so many conventions; it attempts to draw attention to its profundity with such a blind system of borrowings and contrivances, that the work appears constantly threatened by self-parody, and is reflected in itself as if in a distorting mirror. This novel is free of any strictly fantastic material; there are neither ghosts, nor terrifying apparitions, nor inexplicable presences; the fantastic does not lie in what happens to the characters but in their very existence. It would be perfectly possible to imagine a realist version of this novel: a father who inflicts a reign of terror on his family, a mother who is hopelessly weak, children tormented by a wish to be themselves and who vainly try to escape from their grim fate. The "story" is ready to embrace all the meticulous horrors of Naturalism, but the "plot" rejects them. The children's actions are under the control of poetic instinct; they live and move in a frenzy of purity that leads only to their downfall; they cling to moments of paroxysm during which the appearance of things is devastated, and where everything that exists is revealed in the form of stark visions and images.

Dominique Rolin's venture is not without interest, and she devotes a remarkable wealth of emotion and inventiveness to it. But it is quite evident that her book is built on an ambiguity of which she seems unaware, and which consists in presenting to us as if they were the pure products of an illumination, as figures of flame and fury, what nowadays has become mere convention, familiar form, and banal rhetoric. This is not to say that the children she describes owe their existence to Jean Cocteau's *Holy Terrors*, because we do not know whether that is the case, and it is most likely that what she has invented is her own.[5] Nor would we claim that the episode where young Carina finds herself alone in her remote castle is borrowed from *Le grand Meaulnes*, because the question of influence is a mysterious one, and in any case it explains nothing.[6] But there can be no doubt that these inventions, in which Dominique Rolin sees symbols endowed with great expressive power, appear to us as no more than formal paraphernalia that are worn out and ineffective, as conventions whose use is not forbidden, provided they are taken for what they are and not considered as lightning-bolts of pure poetic splendor. The fact is, Dominique Rolin's error is not one that it is easy to avoid. When fantastic literature employs ghosts, mysterious castles, and dreams, it is quite genuinely drawing on resources that tradition has manifestly made conventional, and that are now-adays merely a means for expressing authentic feeling and vision. But if it does without these traditional conventions and claims to express vision and feeling directly, the risk is that it will take feeling itself for a rhetorical device, and make the purity and the sense of the inexpressible that give it its entire reason for existing appear as nothing other than a means to an end. Is it possible to escape this dilemma, and to spare what is the opposite of cliché the indignity of appearing artificial and theatrical? It must be possible, but it calls for a form that is totally sure of itself, and hence a rhetoric that is conscious of the rules that it imposes as the price of the freedom that it grants.

—July 29, 1942

A User's Guide to Montherlant

Bernard Grasset has just published a book by Montherlant that is not entirely by Montherlant, and that leaves it open for him to say, "I am its author," or "I am not its author," as the fancy takes him. In fact, the book is indisputably by him if only because of this ambiguity, the switching between absence and presence, and the dancing around his own shadow thanks to which he shows himself without ever letting himself be caught. What happens if a number of his admirers invite a well-known author to publish a selection of texts taken from his works, with an equally select readership in mind? The writer may refuse, judging that such a choice would compromise the significance of the pages he has written; he may accept, and accept unreservedly, assuming responsibility for this initiative on the part of others as if it came from him; but more subtly than that, he may accept without getting involved, or refuse yet also not stand in the way, and so condone something which does not represent his true thinking. Such has more or less been Montherlant's role in the selection of these texts aimed at younger people, and boasting the fine title *Life Takes the Form of a Prow*.[1]

We are alerted therefore not to see this book as the result of a personal project. It is not the work of Henri de Montherlant as Montherlant might wish the youth of France to read it; there is not even a single page that appears specifically targeted at young French people by its author. Rather, it is a project in which a number of young minds (with the approval of the writer) have highlighted and excerpted what they consider will best serve the interests of the youth of today. Once that is clear, it becomes easier to understand Montherlant's reservations. Even an artist who sets great store by exemplary morals and values will find it difficult to see his art reduced down to the useful elements it contains, to the good use it can be put to or to an external goal which would add something to what it is. An artist cannot tolerate seeing what he does adapted to the specific needs of the social milieu, to customs or to education. What he has written only has meaning for someone who can reap its benefits with no thought of enrichment, or more precisely with the intention of not benefiting from it in any way. The reader who reads in order to profit from his reading is unworthy of what he reads, and is condemned furthermore to read without benefit, since his obsession with utility leads him to debase that which, if he is to encounter it intact, he must refuse to subordinate to any purpose whatsoever, least of all to himself.

If what Montherlant and his collaborators have produced inevitably casts a false light on a work that it is in any case not designed to illuminate, it has the merit of making more visible one or two of the ambiguities of that work, and perhaps some of its originalities too. Pierre Bouchet-Dardenne states in a preface that all of Montherlant's books contain a message, that their role is to convince people and that they are moreover founded on a particular notion of good and evil. Perhaps all of that displays a certain disdain for nuance, but it does bring out clearly what confusion can proliferate when a work that is not meant to be clarified is approached by means of clarity of thought. For example, why place side by side, as if we were dealing with the same idea, the claim that every work by Montherlant contains a message, signifies something that is addressed to others, and the claim that there is in Montherlant's work a precise notion of good and evil? Why, on the grounds that many pages only make sense if we assume they are designed to speak of man to other men, consider that this gives them moral significance, that they prescribe rules of conduct, that they specify the goals toward which, at all times and in all places, thoughts and actions, fantasies and instincts should be directed? These strange slippages are perhaps not entirely attributable to Montherlant's commentators; they com rather from an uncertainty inherent in the texts being commented on, and reveal a degree of negligence on the writer's part when it comes to seeing problems through to the end.

Montherlant's moral preoccupations are clearly apparent, as is his concern not to accept the traditional scale of values as it stands. On the other hand, it is less clear how far the spirit of contestation in him extends, and whether, having refused traditional moral values, he also refuses the traditional way in which morality conceives of value. With what does he counter morality? With remarks whose tone may be violent, but whose range is distinctly limited. Take this, for example: "Many actions that ordinary morality considers innocent may condemn a man irredeemably. But lying, murder, theft and pillaging in time of war do not necessarily condemn a man. He can commit them and still retain his superior characteristics. The life of many men is of no more worth than that of a minnow. Theft can often be excused . . . etc." Or this: "The improvement in human quality [the search for quality is of the essence for Montherlant] has nothing to do with morality—don't confuse them!" But this rejection of ethics, the disdain that abruptly strikes it down, in fact leave the entire sweep of its former dominance intact. The morality that is challenged is merely a certain type of morality:

> For more than a century, and even more so over the last twenty years, our people has been inoculated with a morality which says that

what resists should be called "strained," and what is proud be called "haughty" . . . If you add to that Christianity or its aftermath: humanitarianism, pacifism, a general lack of realism, and also the role given to "affairs of the heart" and a systematic and increasingly marked enfeeblement of the notion of justice, the result is morality, by which I mean the nasty gob of phlegm which is lapped up in schools, newspapers, the radio, the cinema, the dispatch box and the pulpit, and in which our wretched people has been steeped and soused for numerous generations.

It is thus the decline of morality that puts Montherlant off morality. While he rejects shop-girl morality with a superior sneer, he does not seem ready to ask himself if morality is not always shop-girl morality, and after an adjustment or two here and there, he restores full honors and total respect to the tablets of stone he had previously decided simply to shelve.

There are so few signs of a desire to innovate in Montherlant that his morality can seem indistinguishable from the orthodox variety. No doubt he is anti-Christian, no doubt he cultivates loathings that isolate him from a lax and complacent civilization, but deep down he accepts all of the virtues that make for a gentleman, and with a few variations, sets himself the same moral goals as those which have occupied the Platonic world for thousands of years. Courage, citizenship, pride, rectitude, disdain, unselfishness, politeness, gratitude, and generosity all make a demand on us whose scope can perhaps not fully be grasped in the emotional climate of today, but they add or subtract very little when it comes to the invisible civilization that is revered unconsciously by everyone. Perhaps the place devoted to disdain or the importance granted to politeness will surprise minds that are too used to regular forms of morality; perhaps the exclusion of all self-denial and all suffering from the ethical sphere will open up a rather different perspective from the one which the mind's eye is in search of; but after all, the vulgarization of Nietzscheism, of what is simplest in Nietzsche, has long since opened the gates to these changes, and there is nothing here to whisk the soul off in one of those whirlwinds where everything which once supported it, everything it saw as a measure, a rule and an ideal is scattered, shattered and shockingly reduced to naught before its eyes. In addition, Montherlant's morality tolerates goals that are never called into question; patriotism comes naturally to him; a belief in order, and hence in the authority that guarantees order, remains a permanent feature of his nature; friendship, a concern for people, is for him a necessary part of a life governed by generosity. In a word, somewhere there exist a good and an evil that do not disappear with the disappearance of the wretched idols that concealed them, and that judge humans according to the way they adhere to these eternal values.

All of that defines a constant from which the texts never deviate much at all. Yet even though Montherlant's moral preoccupations hardly appear scandalous, and however close they may be to providing examples that it might be useful to offer the youth of an entire people (this undeniably provides a significant guarantee of wisdom), it would be puerile not to see that constantly present in Montherlant's thinking there is an indifference to rules, a decision to pass judgment in the name of something that cannot submit to rigid rules or be expressed by them, and a contestatory ardor that never dims and constantly spurs man on through the moral world that is his lot. What does Montherlant tend to emphasize when outlining his ethical views? Specific values? Stable concepts, destined to become reassuringly permanent? Precisely not: he is only interested in arrangements which are almost without moral complexion, which defy analysis and to which sentiment finds itself uncomprehendingly attuned thanks to an instinct for which, were it to be lacking, no instruction could ever provide a substitute. Montherlant places quality above all else, seeing it as "independent of intelligence, morality, and character," as "a rather indefinable notion," "capable on its own of transfiguring an individual and ranking him with the nobility." And he is relentlessly opposed to everything base and vulgar, to that supreme failing which is capable of corrupting any virtue and which, while compatible with temerity and excess, those least conventional of human exertions, will ultimately deprive them of all worth. Clearly, a man who has been blessed with the gifts of quality and generosity can free himself from ordinary ways of being, or equally well respect them, without these two opposing attitudes displaying any real moral significance; what determines the value of how one behaves is a particular tension between body and soul, a particular way of ringing true when one comes into contact with the world, and not an impersonal adherence to objective rules. In a world where he seldom causes a scandal, in which his inner and outer actions accord with traditionally accepted notions, Montherlant's man carries within him a power of opposition, destruction, and violent horror that very quickly ought to take him beyond the good and evil that he nevertheless respects and even reinforces.

Why then, ready as he is to contest everything, does Montherlant leave the essence of our civilization unscathed? One thing at least is certain: he never fully explores a problem. He declares his morality to be anti-Christian, but it remains tied to Christian morality not only through the objects it protects in common with that morality, but even more so through its glorification of the notion of an ultimate goal, through the ethical salvation that, given the lack of any metaphysical and spiritual salvation, Montherlant does not wish to deprive mankind seriously of. If he rejects an elsewhere, or a beyond situated in some afterlife where men place their hope in consolations that appall him, in the life of the here and now he never truly calls into question the existence of a moral beyond where every being can find the equivalent of salvation, the assurance that, once he has attained this beyond, he has fulfilled his destiny and earned both repose and tranquility. Nietzsche's belief that we should take life for what it is, and not erect an absolute to stand above it and justify it, plays a major role in Montherlant's ethic. "Peace must mean 'living';

it should not be devitalizing. . . . Do not just subsist by using
only part of what is humanly possible, by doing only the mini-
mum required for that, the way the swallow, to maintain its
flight, gives only an occasional slight flap of its wings; but
rather, as a human, exploit what is human to the utmost."
"And let me live all the lives, all the diversity and all the contradictions in the world with intensity and detachment, and
let this be so, because I can do it." But whereas Nietzsche
calls out to a life that is pure and inexplicable, a life without
justification or excuse, a life where the glory of what is perish-
able denies all meaning to teleological relations and to every
"with a view to" of whatever sort, Montherlant cannot sustain
the non-sense that founds what is absolutely tragic, and in a
formula that is not simply a turn of phrase, he attributes to
life itself a goal, a reason, a use-value that reinstates it as a
moral value. "Be capable of everything so as to live everything,
live everything so as to know everything, know everything so
as to understand everything, understand everything so as to
express everything." Similarly, the well-known principle of
alternation is inspired by a clear preference for order and hierarchy, for putting things in their place according to a plan in
which life considered as an absolute no longer has a part to
play. It is a matter of experiencing everything, but not confus-
ing everything, of being successively this then that, but not
both at once, of being versatile in order to use up all the forms
life takes, but not losing one's way or being distracted by the
instantaneous enjoyment of everything. "Ring true in contact
with the world outside," says Montherlant when he defines
quality. But life is not about ringing true. It is as indifferent
to such aesthetic perfection as it is to the moral balance that
the harmonious resolution of alternation ultimately presupposes.

What is perhaps most deeply characteristic of Montherlant's ethic is the role played by solitude in our relations with
others, and the need for genuine communication, without
which man will always remain embroiled in a pointless tragedy. Yet if he is sometimes content with the most superficial,

not to say vulgar expressions (as when he explains in *Service Without Purpose* everything he has done for the people, either by devoting time to church youth clubs, or fighting as a humble soldier or practicing sport or writing *The Sand Rose*), he has also demonstrated serenely and profoundly how two paths are available to people who seek to escape the abjection of a society in ruins: solitary activity or membership of a small clique.[2] In this respect, the pages he entitles "Chivalric Orders" call for serious and rigorous thought. What is secret is constantly linked for him to a concern for others, an awareness of which is assumed by all of his books, either incidentally or by design. It is perfectly true that they contain a message, and that the message is an appeal to others who are meant to hear it. But it is also true that this message cannot really be heard, that it must remain secret, and that its author needs to believe that it will escape the death that would result from its revelation and its vulgarization in minds where it would be no more than a pitiful approximation. Such supreme reserve explains the final sentence of his book: "Others will think that they hear in this book the accents and the language of another world, and that there is no chance—whether hoped for or feared—that these could be heard today." For this he provides the following commentary: "It is not entirely fortuitous that the present book comes to its close with the sentence you are about to read. I am convinced that these pages will find no echo in anyone whatsoever, at least not in my country. And I would add that it seems to me pointless to say why." That is not an expression of frivolous arrogance, but one of fierce solitude, of the jealous intimacy of thought that is decidedly more indomitable than the intimacy of the heart.

—August 12, 1942

Considerations on the Hero

It is a legitimate temptation for the mind to want to compare books as diverse in inspiration and intent as the one which Jacques Benoist-Méchin has devoted to letters sent by soldiers killed in the 1914–18 war, Daniel-Rops's study of Ernest Psichari, and the little book in which Georges Dumézil applies his customary method to an analysis of the legend of Horatius and the Curiatii. These books are not only similar in their subject matter, granting equal place to a study of honor and the military spirit; they are remarkable too for the way they all provide a similar view of the hero, despite clear differences in their observations and their points of view.

The word "hero" becomes comprehensible only once its use has excluded it from the sphere of words, and even excluded the possibility of employing it as a word. In the book he has entitled *What Remains* (Albin Michel), Benoist-Méchin's concern is to show equal respect to all those whose testimony he has collected, and he readily acknowledges that they were all equal in their deeds, since the ultimate one, in which they faced death, meant that each of them met a destiny

that was equally final.[1] Nonetheless, he does show some preference for soldiers who did not even leave a passing trace of
themselves in a private letter, who remained absolutely silent
about themselves and whose anonymity signifies a refusal to
be judged and glorified in the usual ways. There is in the hero
an urge that makes him invisible while nevertheless allowing
him to appear, and that leaves him free for all to see, the way
a statue sometimes is when displayed atop a monument; but
if one comes closer, it turns out that he is not there, and only
a space, an incomprehensible void provide a sign that he exists.
Perhaps all war presupposes that void, without which it is
merely hubbub and commotion, and which gives it a degree
of significance from within.

Benoist-Méchin seems to have been interested above all by
the testimony of those who went to war fully aware of what
it meant for them, and who did not accept its constraints
blindly, but with a clear vision of the extreme experience it
invited them to undergo. Clarification of something as extreme
as this is rarely forthcoming, and only one or two allusions at
most, uttered as if in passing and with a discretion that makes
them all the more precious, give a hint of its presence. There are
moving statements on the subject of the horrors to which the
ordeals imposed by war give rise, and about its intolerable
nature, materially and morally; but these remain too vague
and too bound up with traditional forms to provide a direct
translation of the authentic reality of that horror. The tragic
colors of the soldier's life are usually displayed in response to
an ideal, a patriotic or a religious ideal. He bears the unbearable, or experiences what seemed to lie beyond experience, by
relating them to a nobility and a necessity that justify them
from without, and restore them to the system of things that
exist on a human scale. War, which in itself is dreadful and
absurd, finds in an extrahuman goal a means of becoming the
experience of a natural human possibility. "War is divine,"
said Joseph de Maistre, and by calling it divine he brought it
back down to the level of the ordinary powers and ambitions

of men. It is a scandal, but a scandal that has its rules and its justification, a paradox that dissolves into meaning and law.

Nonetheless, there are some who clearly feel that there is in war a nihilistic fury that consumes whatever close or distant goal that may be given to it. Where does war lead? In what direction? Compared to what it brings, is there any significance in the will to conquer and the hope of a people who resist? The soldier, in the storm that tears him asunder, is henceforth conscious only of something impossible from which, if it comes to it, death may deliver him, but whose nature cannot be comprehended in terms of any of the goals that exist in life. It is no longer a matter of sacrifice in the name of a greater good, nor of a willing sacrifice to nothing, but of an ultimate act which ceases to be a sacrifice or a diminution to the extent that it appears devoid of all efficacy and all justification. "Our error is that we are always working toward something," writes Ferdinand Belmont, one of the men whose testimony is published by Benoist-Méchin. The hero is totally without self-interest, not only because he expects no recompense and has no goal in view that would offer a reward, but also because he is convinced that his great deeds, his great thoughts and his sufferings have no purpose, must have no purpose, and are meaningful only if they are such that, once encountered, all attempts at explaining them appear unjustified and without value.

Whoever takes such an experience as this to its furthest limit can only return from it bearing paradoxical utterances, and the feelings that permit him to live it will of necessity be unusual and surprising. To underline the transfiguring power of war, as Benoist-Méchin does when he analyzes the writings of Pierre-Maurice Masson, Auguste Cochin, Marc Boasson, and Pierre Dupouey; to bring out the gaiety that accompanies people even when they are crushed and their actions lose all meaning, is to impose a name on states that cannot be named, and by so specifying them, make the common situations to which that specification links them appear ridiculous. The joy of the hero in the face of death is no more significant than his dreadful weariness beneath the monotonous blows of an unusual fate, and this torpor bordering on paralysis displays the same "rarefaction of the spiritual atmosphere" (Marc Boasson), the same enhancement of what is human as the sentiment that causes Henri Achalme to say at the moment of his death: "I am happy." "Torpor, slow intoxication, a sleep of the soul," writes Marc Boasson, or else these three words during a battle: "Alive, mad, atrocious." And Léo Latil: "If you think of me constantly, you must feel constant joy, because I am in a constant state of utter peace, and often even gaiety." This pure joy and this lackluster anguish are two signs for the same abnormal passion that, beneath the mask of military glory, accompanies the obscure, free-ranging dreams of a will that refuses to be limited by any object. The fury and the rage that are typical of the ancient warrior express the reality of existence when it is embodied in its most extreme terms, and linked in its entirety to tragedy. It is organized madness placed in the service of an order, whether patriotic or religious, and yet lived internally as delirium, as an irrational and inhuman surplus given to man so that he may find fulfillment.

The interest of Daniel-Rops's study of Ernest Psichari lies in the nature of the preference that his hero showed for war, against all odds.[2] Psichari was the man who wrote these remarkable lines: "The mere idea of war provides us with a thrill of pleasure." This young Christian glorifies war not as a means but as an end, an absolute that momentarily overshadows everything else. The violence that grips his soul in his youth ("I believe that only violent people can be wise people"), the need for discipline that later makes him submit totally to his chosen authority, the equivalence between the religious spirit and the military spirit that, after Joseph de Maistre, he feels deep within himself, make him an exemplary instance of those strong minds for whom war provides a means of responding to destiny (or providence) through action that is free of all the meanness of action. Daniel-Rops interprets and comments on Psichari's declarations in order to tone down their brutality, and it is certainly appropriate to restore to them the religious perspective that Psichari was careful to respect. In the end, however, the fact remains: his unreserved enthusiasm for the violence of war, the impulse that makes him say in 1908, "As someone made for war and yearning for it the way a painter yearns to paint," and write to his mother on August 20, 1914, two days before his death, "I am less than ever repentant at having wished for war," not to mention his belief in the mysterious value of bloodshed, all defy any reasonable outlook and presuppose an image of the world where the tragedy of the call to arms, through its destruction and its divisions, endows communal existence with an obsessive value without which it would be unbearable. Psichari presents the experience of war as the equivalent of a spiritual experience, because in each case, man is placed beyond the reach of the system of motives and ends. The hero discovers in the combat that kills him for no purpose the culmination of a life he has sought to preserve from any particular purpose, while reserving it for that pinnacle of purposelessness: grandeur.

At various points in his interpretation of the legend of Horatius, *Horatius and the Curiatii*, Georges Dumézil focuses on the principle of heroic force that is generally represented, among the Indo-European peoples, through myths of a warlike character.[3] The aim of this learned comparativist is to find in the story of Horatius's combat not so much the trace of a historical event, but an adaptation of a myth designed to represent an ancient military initiation rite. Irish legends reveal to us the initiatory exploits of Cuchulainn on the day he receives his arms. The king's young nephew must combat three adversaries; he overcomes them, and this triple victory plunges him into a state of frenzy that transforms him and endows him with incomparable worth. But as a result of this fury, he becomes a danger even for his own family. He must therefore undergo a purification and be made, in a precise sense, to cool down. Accordingly, the king forces him to contemplate lewd women before whom he is forced to lower his eyes, before plunging him into vats of cold water where his ardor is cooled. The legend of Horatius reproduces the main outlines of these episodes. The young Horatius too wins a victory over a triple adversary; he too, on returning to the city, meets a lewd female relative of his, whose provocative behavior appears intolerable to the angry man he has become through combat; finally, the authorities must restore him to the society of men by means of a calming, purifying medication, and while preserving all the benefits of his initiation, free him from the peril and defilement into which his exceptional state has plunged him.

Georges Dumézil provides a minute examination of the differences separating the two legends, and he explains them by showing how Roman mythology, through eliminating the element of the marvelous from the ancient rite, transformed it into a romance and retained only its outlines, which is to say the same framework of fact, but justified by reasons that were both psychological and judicial. That element of the marvelous is provided by the acquisition of warlike fury, the magic power that the Teutons call *wut*, the Irish *ferg*, and to which the word *furor* corresponds in the Latin language. It is a "transfiguring" frenzy, a heightened state that changes man into a tireless, unfeeling, even invulnerable hero. By means of the delirium that brings him into contact with the stormy elements of nature, the warrior becomes, in Marie-Louise Sjoestedt's words, "a madman, possessed by his own tumultuous, burning energy."[4] He is Ajax, Achilles, or Hector, consumed by anger and plunged into a state where the common rules of humanity no longer have any meaning. The Greek *menos* accurately expresses this impetuousness, this violence that not only incites delirious passions in men but also alters the course of rivers, turns breath into a hurricane and fire into an incendiary ardor that nothing can contain or assuage. Among the Latins, for whom military valor depends more on science and discipline than on the daring of a single individual, "furor" is represented by the exploits of a figure such as Horatius Cocles, who can put his enemies to flight simply by looking at them, and by the young Horatius, who in his victorious frenzy refuses to accept that humanity can devote itself to anything other than combat.

These are familiar images, drawn from a dream that is experienced in the midst of action. "It is pathetic to behold the multifarious yet monotonous effort on the part of humanity to go beyond itself without ever leaving its existing order, but rather by simply disrupting its rhythm, condensing its energy into illusory performance and seeking to breach the contours or earthly limits which have been given to it," writes Georges Dumézil. But the hero is witness to a doubly impossible ambition, since if he wishes to go further than he has the power to, he also wants to find in the exercise of his power the ecstasy and the supreme dignity that only the refusal of action can provide—what in the West is called contemplation and in the East not-knowing [*non-savoir*]. On the one hand, he seeks to go beyond the possible by becoming the man of the unachievable act; and on the other, he purports to seek from some great act the same illumination, the same pure apotheosis as those promised by the tireless quest for nonaction. In *Ecce Homo*, Nietzsche defined the nature of his "warrior instinct" as follows: "My way of waging war can be summed up in four points. First: I only attack causes that are victorious—I may even wait until they become victorious. Second: I only attack causes against which I would find no allies, so that I stand alone—so that I compromise myself alone. . . . Third, I never attack persons. . . . Fourth: I only attack things when all personal differences are excluded, when any background of bad experiences is lacking. On the contrary, to attack is to me a proof of goodwill."[5] Such are the demands of the hero, but they are borrowed here from an entirely spiritual order, and already turned against the action whose excellence they claim to determine. The hero feels within himself the contradiction that decrees that, by wishing to take as the model for his experience of violence a moral attitude that is free of the prejudices of violence, he only ever wins one victory: his death, which is a middle term between "practice" and meditation, the meeting point of day and night.

—September 9, 1942

"The Finest Romantic Book"

The story of Bettina and Goethe has long appeared as one of the most brilliant stories that Romanticism provides. The love of a mysterious child, as lively and acerbic as a flame, for the august old man who had already entered posterity and become his own imperishable statue; that union of what was most elemental and ardent in nature with the enduring sovereignty of the mind and its order, that reincarnation of Mignon in the guise of a veritable female kobold, who made the seductive star of sensibility gleam for one last time in a firmament that was too sublime: such an episode was inevitably destined to become a magnificent symbol, and replete with multiple meanings, to remain the epitome of a story that is finer in its reality than any literary fiction.

But it eventually became clear that this story was, precisely, no more than a fiction that had been marvelously organized and embellished by Bettina herself. The celebrated work entitled *Goethe's Correspondence with a Child*, which Bettina published in 1835 and which is considered (rather too kindly) to be the finest German Romantic book, has been superseded by the actual correspondence between Bettina and Goethe, which remained almost unknown until 1922, when Fritz Berge-mann's edition was published, and which has just now appeared in a translation by Jean Triomphe.[1] These documents, which incidentally are often very fine, reveal to their reader how cunningly and how ingeniously the "Child" cast a veil of lies over the facts; and how, as well as publishing her own letters to Goethe and Goethe's actual replies, she also added new pages, concocted imaginary scenes, embellished the poet's notes to her, and transformed into words of affection and flattering confidences the requests for a favor, the expressions of thanks, or the words of advice that generally provide the sole contents of the letters she receives. Her aim was manifestly to show that she had had a profound influence on the life of the aging Goethe, providing the inspiration for some of his works and bringing a last ray of warming sunshine to a heart frozen inside its memories. But history shows that she left no trace whatsoever on that life, and that though he was perhaps touched by this enthusiastic creature, Goethe soon had only one thing in mind: to respond with ever-greater reserve to her tiresome whims.

Stripped once and for all of its enchantment, this relationship nonetheless remains extremely interesting thanks to Bettina's own nature, and for the way it illustrates the extraordinarily clumsy manner in which this otherwise highly intelligent and astute girl set about conquering a great mind that she had placed on the defensive. Bettina had two cards up her sleeve, and they were far from negligible. She was the daughter of Maximiliane La Roche, to whom Goethe had sworn eternal friendship, and in Frankfurt she had become the close friend, confidante, and effectively a daughter to Goethe's mother. A first meeting took place between them in the spring of 1807. Bettina has left the most fanciful accounts of this event, claiming (she alludes to this in one of her letters) that she rested her head on the poet's shoulder and fell asleep there; Goethe, on the other hand, merely notes this encounter in his diary with the words "Mam'selle Brentano." In the autumn there is a second meeting, during which Goethe appears to have granted Bettina one or two favors, since he allows her to address him using the "*du*" form and to embrace him. For over three years, letters of extraordinary passion whose inspired ardor seems inexhaustible follow on from this incipient idyll, and Goethe replies to them with the most dignified courtesy and a clear concern for propriety. But nothing can discourage young Bettina, who sees Goethe for a third time in 1810, then a fourth time a year later, by which time she has become Frau von Arnim. This last encounter has disastrous consequences for her passion. A scene (in which jealousy no doubt plays a part) occurs between her and Christiane von Goethe, who loses her temper and in her agitation, breaks her rival's spectacles. It is the end of a beautiful dream. Goethe uses the scandal as an excuse to turn a deaf ear from now on to such indiscreet and chaotic sentiment. Bettina continues to send fine, pathetic letters now and then, but in spite of the brief reconciliation that occurs fifteen years later, the note written by Goethe in his diary for August 7, 1830—"Rebuffed Frau von Arnim's importuning"—provides the key to their true relationship.

Bettina's letters reveal that the girl hopes to seduce the man she has made into her god with the sort of behavior that is most likely to make him impatient and hostile. Such a ploy has a sort of absurd charm about it. Everything that can possibly annoy Goethe and make him wish for this mad venture to end—not only excessive capriciousness and delirious excitability, but also the monotony of sterile devotion, constant ravings that are both intemperate and incoherent, a lack of discernment and even tact, in short this entire system of covertly contrived enthusiasm—is flaunted by Bettina at every turn as proof of what ought to bring her glory and favor her courtship. Seemingly insensitive to the bother she inflicts on Goethe, she develops to their utmost the qualities that make her unbearable, and distorts those features that could have earned her a hard-won friendship. She is nothing but sensibility in turmoil, childlike excitement, and a feverish passion that consumes and warps everything. Her sense of what is grand and noble, her engaging intelligence, and her petulant yet amiable spirit degenerate into a lyricism that trifles with reality and constantly replaces it with a dream whose untruth delights her. Even more remarkable is the fact that such a gifted spirit could be so blind not only to Goethe's character, but to the nature and significance of Goethe's art. She generally sends him remarks such as this: "When I saw you for the first time, what struck me and inspired in me a profound veneration and a profound love was that your entire person expresses what David said about men: each must be a king unto himself, that is to say, the inner nature of man must prevail over uncertainty and the randomness of the outer world." Such words, by making the whim of an individual soul the law of poetic inspiration, could not be further removed from Goethe's unvarying view. In the same way, Bettina constantly extols dream as a source of poetry: "Is a dream nothing?" she says to him. "For me, it is everything." Or else: "During the summer, amidst the eternal and impassioned life of all the colors, at the moment when man partakes of supreme beauty with a profound sympathy, it often seems to him that he himself is like a dream which vanishes like a perfume before the light of reason." And that is said to the writer who always mistrusted dreams, and whose response to Arnim's poetry was the telling reproach that it had a "tendency to dream."

With the enthusiasm that makes her love in Goethe not what he is exactly, but an image of all that is superior and creative, and that makes her want to be loved for qualities Goethe can find only detestable, Bettina remains as it were the symbol of those young Romantics who vainly sought to be understood by the being whose glory so inspired them, and whom, while welcoming them generously and kindly, Goethe derides in Act I of *Faust*, dubbing them "poets of the night and the graveyard." In the sentimental frenzy of this impassioned dreamer who, capricious inconstancy incarnate and yet with incredible fidelity, haunts that great genius of plasticity and is constantly rejected and yet constantly finds reason to hope; in all this unparalleled stubbornness there is so to speak an image of the urge that drives the most formless nocturnal visions, the most obscure and indecipherable enigmas, in short all that is unreal in Romantic lyricism, toward a law of such visibly harmonious form. Bettina is the messenger whom Brentano, Arnim, and Hoffmann dispatch to the poet of poets, the great universal being who possesses every faculty of understanding and yet who disavows them nonetheless, because he sees in the literature of this new generation a bastard creation, one which is without contour and as elusive as treasures that lie buried at the bottom of the sea. As her entire story shows, Bettina in fact failed to fulfill that embassy with which history had unconsciously entrusted her, leaving Goethe merely with an impression of her extravagance, irresponsibility, and dishonesty. But it is also true that she herself succeeded in deceiving history, by replacing the truth with the legendary image of the aged Goethe, experiencing the joys of love for one last time in the declarations and endearments of an enigmatic little demon. Indeed, that is so true that every critical attempt at a rectification will probably remain powerless to dispel the illusions she succeeded in establishing.

The symbolic role that Bettina played is all the more striking in that her love for Goethe is inseparable from Arnim's deep love for her. How far was the unyielding passion felt first by the girl, then by the woman for the old man of Weimar endured by Arnim as "a veritable mystical betrayal," as André Breton puts it in a study of the author of the *Bizarre Tales*?[2] Or on the contrary, was Arnim so sure of being loved that he never took umbrage at Goethe's letters, as Albert Béguin believes? Leaving aside such anecdotal mysteries, what remains is the dramatic sacrifice made by a young poet who was still unknown to a great and illustrious poet, a sacrifice that is not a matter of love itself perhaps, but rather of the most juvenile and delightful expressions of love that literature has ever invented. Whatever may have been Arnim's confidence in Bettina, it is not with him but with Goethe that these confessions of unparalleled sensibility, these mementos of the heart that will survive even their own imposture, remain associated. It was to Goethe, not Arnim, that these incomparable words were addressed: "Deep in the night, surrounded by perspectives that belong to my youth, with all the sins you always accuse me of, and which I confess to, behind me, and before me the heaven of reconciliation, I seize the cup with its nocturnal draught, I drain it to your wellbeing, and seeing the dark brilliance of the wine on its crystal rim, I think of your most beautiful eyes." Of that at least, Arnim, the generous, noble Arnim was deprived, resigning himself to never seeing his name joined with that of his wife in the eyes of posterity, and accepting this sacrifice seemingly without bitterness, out of gratitude toward the great genius whom he revered. But for his part, faithful to the point of injustice to his solemn mission, Goethe nevertheless continues to reject young poets and condemn all Romanticism, indeed condemning Arnim himself with these implacable words: "By nature, feminine; in substance, fanciful; content, insubstantial; composition, limp; form, floating; effect, illusory." This judgment sweeps the new literature aside as completely as Goethe swept Bettina herself aside in a letter to Karl August: "This insufferable gadfly whom my mother bequeathed me has been a regular nuisance for a number of years."

Thus the failure of the "Child," of the woman Goethe's mother called "the girl with an imagination like a skyrocket," would have been unmitigated had she not found a vengeance in the eyes of history that not even the truth could deprive her of. This victory cannot be put down simply to a misunderstanding. Rather, it is Bettina's character, her chameleon-like instinct and the power she had to impose on others the grand and powerful imaginings that convulsed her, that all render this outcome authentic. As several critics have remarked, it was not out of mere vanity or a morbid need to be admired that she allowed herself to follow in the wake of great artists and, like a dancer, without warning, to throw them a bouquet after executing each figure. In fact, she is in search of something more profound, which she occasionally glimpses in her dreams and then attempts to discover in human society. Both Goethe and Beethoven are an image of the truth and the treasures that the night reveals in her and that the waking hours conceal. "To be an element imbued with powers of a higher nature" is what she expects from her wild bouts of admiration, because she has experienced the joy of it in dreams where, in her words, she had the impression that "her inner being welcomed her into itself with love." Like Ludwig Tieck, like Jean Paul, like all of Romanticism she cries: "O my dreams, why do you live? O my life, why do you not live?" And she asks Goethe to embody this dream, to transform her life into a fundamental harmony in which thoughts, actions, and sentiments form the echo of the most beautiful night. Yes, she indeed had her vengeance, and vengeance on Goethe himself, since she forced the great genius of plasticity to appear before history as the shadow-laden dream and slumber of her inspired and whimsical little soul.

—September 16, 1942

That Infernal Affair

The infernal affair in question is the strange story of the relations between Jean-Jacques Rousseau and David Hume. Henri Guillemin, who is well known for his excellent work on Lamartine, is the latest to take up the story of this incredible and heinous episode, and he has produced a truly novel book, *That Infernal Affair*, which is informed by precise and accurate analysis, and is so totally convincing that it would command our full assent, were it not sometimes too glibly persuasive and too eager to overcome our resistance.[1]

In the dispute between Hume and Rousseau, Guillemin sees much more than a petty personal affair in which two great men with little to agree about, having duped each other with an illusory friendship, found all their faults exposed. In Hume he identifies a tool of the Encyclopedists who used him to attack their mortal enemy, the man who had written the "Profession of Faith of a Savoyard Vicar" and who believed in Christianity. That was an episode in a struggle during which, rightly considering himself to be the victim of persecution, Rousseau ultimately found that this was less the case than he thought, and through his extravagance, provided proof of the accusation of madness that his enemies had initially brought against him unjustly. Hume administers the unkindest cut of all by pretending to like him, then denouncing him when the time comes in a welter of malice and recrimination.

Guillemin gives a lengthy account of how the Philosophers schemed against Rousseau, men he calls "the brothers" after the name one of their number gave them, and he is in no doubt that Voltaire, Diderot, d'Alembert, Grimm, and Holbach would stop at nothing to drive their adversary mad or render him helpless. He gives little weight to personal grudges. The hate shown by this clique is philosophical in nature. The person who had written, "Yes, if the life and death of Socrates were those of a sage, the life and death of Jesus were those of a God," could not be shown any amicable indulgence. He must be brought low. Cunning, violence, calculated malice, and barefaced insult are all considered fair means for bringing about his destruction. There is a permanent plot against this feeble creature.

Hume plays a role in this extraordinary conspiracy. He is a skeptic, an atheist at bottom, a "brother" himself and in complete agreement with those who are determined to destroy Jean-Jacques. When he invites Rousseau to England for the first time, he thinks that as a writer the latter is on the right side, though he quickly realizes his mistake; he thinks he is serving the cause; he wishes both to be friendly toward a man of renown, and to rescue a philosopher who is an ally from persecution by the civil authorities. A stay in Paris reveals his error, and he would have withdrawn his invitation had not Mme de Verdelin and Mme de Boufflers insisted he renew it, and even obliged him hastily to organize a trip that he no longer wishes to make. He therefore puts a good face on it. On the surface, he is Jean-Jacques's best friend. He praises him, serves him, and tends to his needs; but in fact he is observing him, spying on him, laughing at him sometimes, and indulging some of his own wicked designs. Jean-Jacques is initially taken in, but gradually he begins to see a hypocrite in the friend he thought he had found. He is frightened by his own suspicions. He cannot forgive himself for having such a poor opinion of someone he had so wished to like. On March 18, 1766, in an incredible scene, having caught Hume indiscreetly about to read his letters and accused him of the worst in his heart, he throws himself at Hume's feet in tears and tells him of his doubts, thus revealing indirectly that he has found him out and no longer has any confidence in his deceitful friend. From that moment on, Hume is determined to provoke a violent row, and he arranges everything so that the wrong should all be on Rousseau's side and so that philosophy should benefit from the quarrel. He plots, he schemes, he lies. He artfully snares the wretched Jean-Jacques with the pension he receives from the king of England; he finally forces him to break off relations and replies to him with a little book on which all the philosophers collaborate, and which he distributes with the aim of being the most spiteful and implacable of adversaries. And indeed, upset at having been deceived by such affection, Rousseau leaves England in a state of frenzy that he manages to overcome only a few months before his death.

Henri Guillemin brings out all the details of this story in an analysis that is pursued with patience and honesty as well as with passion. He loves truth, and he loves Jean-Jacques. Above all, he loves the faith that Rousseau bears witness to and against which the cold and cruel inventors of anti-Christian rationalism conspire, with an extreme and hateful violence to which they devote all of their thinking. The affair is an "infernal" one because in the persecution of a man who will eventually succumb to it there is something malevolent and relentless, a talent for torment that is quite inordinate, a pleasure in causing pain which trivial passions cannot sufficiently explain. "Their burning hatred, immortal as the Demon who inspires it," Rousseau wrote in his *Reveries*. Guillemin does not seem to take these words figuratively, and he implies that hell may well have had a hand in this quarrel, which at all events cannot be reduced to a simple matter of vanity among writers.

What continues to cloud the issue in a story that becomes clearer once the documents are examined yet still remains contentious, is the fact that it appears to be true at several levels, and depending on the angles from which it is viewed, it displays nuances of interpretation that cannot easily be discounted. Guillemin readily considers it from Jean-Jacques's point of view. Sometimes he even appears to have total faith in Jean-Jacques's account of it, correcting it only in order to widen its significance, and take in the full range of the perils that it perceives and describes only in a piecemeal fashion. He is thus in no doubt that there was indeed a plot and a conspiracy, a dastardly plot and a conspiracy that was marvelously contrived so as to destroy a man and make him mad. On the other hand, he has difficulty attributing to Hume ulterior motives that the English philosopher seems only to have been clearly aware of almost three months after Jean-Jacques's arrival in London. For the plot to have been real, for Rousseau's accusations to be proven ("I had been lured to England on account of a project which was beginning to form, but whose purpose I was ignorant of"), it would be necessary to see in Hume's invitation the most appalling stratagem for sequestrating a guest, in every action of the English writer an attempt at taking advantage of ingenuousness before driving it to despair, and in that candid friendship a fiction designed to bring about a break and make it appear as proof of inconstancy and ingratitude. All that is impossible to prove, and Guillemin only does so partially. It is more accurate to say that he often tends very sensibly, particularly in his conclusion, toward a more moderate version and gives David Hume a role that makes him more of an ally than a conspirator. But sometimes, in the course of analyses that make him prove more than he wants to, he also gives the impression that Hume really is at the center of machinations over which he does have control; he paints him as black as Rousseau saw him; he suspects him as much for his lavish praise as for his unstinting services. He transforms him into a monstrous impostor with a genius for cruelty.

The emotional duplicity of the English philosopher, his lack of interest in a friendship that does not lie or mock the friend, last of all his concern, once the break is imminent, to exploit it in a way that will serve his reputation, are all things that are undeniably true. But is it not fair to say that Rousseau too was driven to adopt a certain duplicity of attitude in response to a quite different instinct? If from the outset Hume makes fun at the expense of the man on whom he lavishes a great show of cordiality, Rousseau readily embraces someone whom he is not far from mistrusting, and to whom in his soul, troubled—or enlightened—as it is by the night, he attributes the famous words "I have, I have Jean-Jacques Rousseau." Later, when he already considers Hume to be a traitor, he goes on loving him and weeps at the knees of man whose perfidy is no longer in any doubt. He can still write to him: "I embrace you and love you with all my heart." He also denounces him to Mme de Verdelin: "You absolutely must know the truth about the David Hume to whom you delivered me," and yet he still continues openly to be his friend and his debtor. His correspondent is so acutely aware of this ambivalence that she discreetly reproaches him for it: "If you have revealed your suspicions to other people as well as me, I wonder if I should not advise you to declare them to him yourself." In these relations between Hume and Rousseau, the friendship that is so vocally to the fore is accompanied by a reciprocal wariness, an exchange of suspicions that taints them from the outset. But whereas Hume displays duplicity out of natural unscrupulousness, as well as fanatical self-interest perhaps, Rousseau appears ambiguous through an excess of sensibility, but also perhaps of sincerity. Hume puts on an act with Rousseau; Rousseau puts on an act with himself. His soul is torn between unstinting friendship and suspicion that withholds even the most basic esteem; with one hand he gives his heart and with the other withdraws his confidence. He cannot prevent himself from seeing a blackguard in the person he wishes he could love as a paragon, and in this dual judgment that is equally excessive on both sides, he sinks deeper into torment and eventually becomes unbalanced.

What makes this affair so painful and impenetrable is that it is impossible to know if it is the cause of Jean-Jacques's delirium or already one of its early effects. The rumor that Rousseau was mad was the great invention of the Encyclopedists. They said or wrote a hundred times: he is a savage beast, a dangerous madman. They portrayed him as unstable, distrustful, with a compulsion to accuse his best friends. They presented him as more incapable of affection the more he was in need of it. "The friend of all men" is their friend only in order that he may reject them. Such are the familiar and typical claims of the Philosophers. Thus when, after a first few weeks of untroubled intimacy, Hume begins to murmur that his guest is perhaps rather sensitive, that he sometimes has fits of melancholy ("he is like a man who has been stripped not only of his clothes, but of his skin"), Guillemin can justifiably argue that the Englishman has lent his voice to the chorus of the "brothers," revealing his complicity by adopting their usual descriptions. But what happens a little later on? Jean-Jacques really starts to resemble the man the Encyclopedists portrayed; he suspects and maltreats not only his enemies but also those who are most loyal to him; he accuses his cousin Jean of being "the damned soul of good King David"; he accuses the painter Ramsay of giving him the face of a "Cyclops" in order to make him look guilty of every depravity; he calls the Comtesse de Boufflers and the Marquise de Verdelin two "furies" who are dogging his steps. Finally, he succumbs to the delirium so many books have described, and that he confesses to at the beginning of the *Reveries* in 1776: "A delirium that took no less than ten years to calm down." Is it possible that the man who believed he was a prey to illusory persecution and who denounced all sorts of imaginary intrigue could also have been the victim of real plots and real persecution? Could only a perfidious mind suspect a man who was destined to succumb to nightmare of being of a somber, melancholy humor? Was it a calumny to describe as oversensitive the man who would soon write, "Where can I go? Where can I hide? Where can I find safer shelter from my enemies? Where will they not find me? They are after my life." But such is the drama peculiar to Jean-Jacques: the enemies he invents make us doubt the real and implacable enemies he has; the plots he invents conceal the scheming of those who seek to attack him, and the truly melancholic aspects of his character justify the supposed misanthropy that so many minds set on harming him say is his. There is something distressing about this passion, which condemns the victim of persecution to become so acutely aware of his own misfortunes that he makes them unbelievable even though they are quite undeniable, and which turns him into the plaything of fantasized plots because he fears too intensely the serious plots that are destroying him. When someone slides imperceptibly from truth to delusion, he ceases entirely to be believed while only partly ceasing to be truthful. In that respect, the history of Romanticism and the history of Jean-Jacques coincide.

—September 23, 1942

Vigils of the Mind

Perhaps the rate at which books about philosophy are published need not appear as regular, monotonous, and inevitable to the reader as in the case of novels or works of criticism.[1] A sort of reverence rooted in tradition expects them always to be exceptional, and to depend on such extraordinary conditions that they can only ever appear in very small numbers, and at irregular intervals. It is difficult to accept that philosophy is destined to be read. It is therefore not unpleasant to see so few volumes of a strictly philosophical nature listed among the works that have recently appeared. The sole signs of activity that deserve our attention are provided by two fine books by Brice Parain on language, which it will be possible to discuss once the official critics on the thesis jury have had their say; a number of studies on mysticism and psychoanalysis to which we intend to return; and finally, a new collection by Alain and a study of psychology considered as a behavioral science by Pierre Naville.

Alain's book may well appear unnecessary to those who think they know Alain. The hundred remarks collected there with the title *Vigils of the Mind* are already present in people's memories, and together they epitomize a manner of thinking that many a mind can now identify as that of Alain, thanks to almost forty books, an illustrious career as a teacher, and dialogues that are constantly being renewed.[2] *Elements of Philosophy* recently gave us the opportunity to examine this great and powerful mind, in which the influence of a teacher, the action of a journalist and the prestige of an exceptional writer are successfully combined.[3] What does his latest book add to his thinking, as once again it sets about weaving and unpicking its strands, and on every subject, as is his wont, obliging the mind to admit that it knows less than it thinks, and showing it to be a figure of clay, perfect yet already reduced to dust, and molded from a material in which no form can ever endure? Nothing perhaps, or perhaps everything. How can a philosophy be criticized for constantly returning to the same idea, if the only lesson it claims to offer us is the impossibility of considering that idea, or indeed any idea, as definitive?

Alain's intellectual habits can easily be summed up in two sentences, for which Alain himself provides the wording: "To think without an object is vain," he says, "but to handle and explore an object without thought is another sort of foolishness." That is the trace of Cartesian rationalism that survives within the twin perspectives that Plato and Hegel provide him with. Experience and reason, taken separately, do not simply amount to nothing; but if the fact is missing or badly observed, thought is no more than bravura whose outcome is dream; and fact reduced solely to itself leads nowhere except to sleep, in which we think we have reached the truth, whereas we are sleeping and so can grasp nothing. Those are the maxims that always come to mind as soon as Alain appears and starts to reel off his thoughts, and often as not, they seem narrow and simple. Narrow no doubt, like everything that allows reason to reign too freely; but not simple, or rather never simple enough, since in order for them to be intelligible they have constantly to be revived, and once they are totally clear they are worse than nothing: an empty gleam that beguiles and deceives the eye.

The countless brief studies that Alain devotes to everyday objects and to objects of everyday or contemporary history have, it could be said, tended to remain meaningful and to breathe new life into those two maxims not so much by preserving them as such, as by preventing them from being maxims at all, which is to say by striking them with countless blows on the understanding that, constantly destroyed and constantly renewed, they were for the lazy mind a discovery that was always new, an endless subject of astonishment and enlightenment. In certain respects, the sole content of Alain's philosophy is provided by his thought as he exercises it. In contact with the experience of each day he must think and constantly rethink the principles he recognizes: as principles laid down once and for all in language, they signify merely the death of the mind that they seek to bring to life; they encourage a false sense of security; they supply props where any sort of support would be too ponderous; they are the opposite of what they are. They should therefore only be grasped within the thinking where they acquire their sense and their value. Alain must think them if they are to become principles that are valid for everyone. As soon as a book makes them permanent, they deserve mistrust and suspicion. And if speech is better suited to them, they require the sort of language that is murmured inwardly rather than declaimed. That is what makes Alain's philosophy inseparable by nature from teaching. It also explains the fact that his books are always in search of the same truths and give the impression that they repeat themselves, whereas they continually start afresh and refashion themselves, because the truth cannot be repeated.

In the observations that make up *Vigils of the Mind*, some of which are very well known, all these requirements are clearly in evidence. The primary power of the mind is its power of contestation. It encompasses an indefatigable presence that never rests, is never content, and encounters itself only as that which cannot be there. It is in the nature of an idea to offer whoever grasps it a pure point of contact where, for a second, darkness is dispelled. It belongs only to the one who contests it and tests it at the very moment he encounters it. It urges him to say no to it, for it is in this no, momentarily suspended, that it is affirmed and becomes distinct. It shines thanks to the opposition that the mind shows toward it and that makes it completely present to itself, in the instant in which it is seen by the mind. And it becomes no more than a semblance, if, through being too complete, its victory beguiles thought and transforms its approval into enduring acquiescence. Alain has provided the mind's need to be always on the watch with images and expressions which have become classic because they retain their capacity to stimulate. "Truth is momentary for us shortsighted humans. It belongs to a situation or an instant; it must be seen, said and done at that precise moment, neither before nor after, in ridiculous maxims; and not several times, for nothing exists several times." Or else: "A fool is not so much a man who is mistaken as a man who repeats truths without having first been mistaken, the way those who discovered them were. That is why our predecessors, especially the most ancient among them, who were mistaken about many things, remain good guides; and it is precisely because we cannot be content with what they said that what they said is good." And finally this wonderful image, which must be grasped in all its twists and turns, an image that is continuous and yet renews itself as it develops, one that is simple yet multifaceted:

> Men who sincerely wish to think often resemble the silkworm, which attaches its thread to everything around it and does not see that its brilliant web quickly becomes solid, dry and opaque; that it veils things and will soon conceal them; that this secretion overflowing with light nevertheless creates a dark night and a prison around it; that the worm is weaving its own tomb with threads of gold, so that all that remains for it to do is to sleep, an inert chrysalis providing amusement and adornment for others but of no use to itself. In the

same way, men who think often fall sleep in the necropolis of their systems; and they sleep on, cut off from the world and from mankind; they sleep while others unwind their golden thread and deck themselves out with it.

It is quite clear that this rationalism is sustained through being constantly put to the test, in a manner that makes it appear always to be in thrall to nihilism, which it avoids only thanks to the modesty of its outlook and its hatred of all systems. To say and believe that "everything is vain, everything should be contested" is to be confined within such a vague and general way of thinking that at the very most it can be grasped as a formula, but never as a thought. "I am fortunate," says Alain, "not to believe in what I say at all; such doubt cures one of doubting." For as he is never sure of knowing fully what he knows, or of embracing it other than in through a mechanical form of certainty, he contests it better by learning it rather than by denying it. Thus, he says, "How could ever I stop being a Euclidian, if I cannot even manage to be a Euclidian, by which I mean: be a Euclidian the way one is a Catholic?" Which means perhaps that skepticism exists only where there is belief, and that thought can only become an object or a pretext for belief if it is too vast and too remote from things to be constantly tested and provoked. It should be noted that vigilance of the mind as it is shown to us here is not the expression of an inner dialectic, of the sort whose perpetual exhaustiveness, unceasing movement and uncompromising refusal are enough to ensure that it runs along smoothly. Alain's mind has its own capacity for vigilance, namely judgment, but it also needs experience to awaken it and facts without which its vigils would be no more than brilliant and solitary fantasies; to go from an idea to a fact, then from the fact to an idea in which the fact endures while the idea is renewed by it in return: that is the endless movement that expresses the vigor of the mind when it escapes the clutches of the sleep merchants. In other words, the mind is vigilant only within the experience that governs it, and that cannot govern it unless it understands it. Clearly, since this vigilance is only exercised within the domain of things and with their aid, it comes up short before the whys by means of which the mind itself calls itself into question; it preserves the mind from the supreme interrogation toward which it is nonetheless drawn and that, in the face of discursive knowledge, the absolute knowledge that is the goal of Hegel's enquiry, signifies: What's the use? It holds the mind back at the edge of night and, "in contact with these waking shadows," is transformed for once into sleep, so that the mind itself should not become separated, in this ultimate act, from its condition and its essence, because of the power of desperate clarity that it possesses.

From a certain standpoint, psychology as represented by the science of behavior or behaviorism also consists of a fundamental calling into question, both of consciousness and of every aspect of the psyche. Pierre Naville's recent work *Psychology, the Science of Behavior*, is the first complete account of behaviorist thinking, a doctrine that has been extensively developed in America and to which the name of J. B. Watson remains attached.[4] In France, Henri Pierron, Henri Wallon, and Paul Guillaume have paid some attention to these studies, without, however, accepting all of their principles. The starting point for behaviorism is simple. Whereas traditional psychology, that of William James or Henri Bergson, derives its object and some of its methods from the existence of consciousness, the science of behavior denies introspection and calls on psychology to study everything that is objectively observable in humans in a scientific manner. This principle is categorical. Not only must science stop dealing with states of consciousness, because, as they cannot be the object of experimental observation, they cannot therefore be known; even to go on maintaining the existence of mental events and psychic realities is unacceptably outdated. There are no such things as psychological phenomena: in man as in animals, there are only movements, that is to say, stimuli and reactions to these stimuli.

Although behaviorism does not claim to offer a comprehensive explanation of the facts of human existence, it describes them and seeks to account for them by explaining them as a series of reflexes and conditioned reflexes. The well-known experiments by Pavlov and Bechterew with conditioned reflexes, linking certain glandular and muscular reactions to new stimuli, have provided behavioral science with the main framework for all of its deductions. Just as, in the classic example, a dog that secretes a few drops of saliva when offered a piece of meat will also salivate, in the absence of a piece of meat, if it hears a particular sound that was associated with the stimulus during earlier experiments, in the same way a man who blinks when a bright light is brought closer will blink when he hears an electric bell, then when hearing a certain word or seeing a certain image, provided these different stimuli have been suitably linked by substitution to the original one. All other human reactions, whether emotional like the ones we call fear, anger, or love, or else related to higher functions such as memory or reasoning, are nothing other than sensorimotor processes occurring in the nerves or glands, and are of the same type as conditioned reflexes. Thought, for example, is the process of talking to oneself, and speech, whether internal or explicit, can be entirely explained by the increasingly complex conditioning that establishes in the child, as it grows up, an equivalence of reaction toward words and things. The significance of speech thus presupposes no mysterious reality; it is the reaction that, among all the ways of reacting to an object, an individual will necessarily display at a specific moment and in a given situation. "Meaning," says J. B. Watson, "is just one way of telling what an individual is doing."[5]

Behaviorism naturally provoked considerable criticism. But it is remarkable most of all for the vigorous nature of the presuppositions and the firmness of the assumptions to which its rigorously scientific claims have given rise. For in the name of what can it be decided that mental states do not exist? What experiments can be cited so as to make such negative certainty unshakable, and make it possible not just to deny that psychic phenomena are valid syndromes, but to deny that they are phenomena at all? In order to establish itself as a science, behaviorism was obliged to sacrifice considerable scientific caution; so as to give total priority to experimental control, it had to base itself on a principle that cannot be proved experimentally; before becoming the realm of calculated observation and strict formulation, it could only evolve a sort of theology, made up of theses and doctrine. (In Naville's book we come across remarks of this sort: "The behaviorist point of view must be accepted as a principle.") And if it is evident that the contestation of consciousness is perhaps not without its use, even from the standpoint of the strange formation that is part art and part physics and that we call psychology, that contestation must be such that, in its turn, it is constantly turned against itself, constantly revealing what it signifies, what it attacks, what it ensures, and on what ignorance it depends—all of which are questions that must indefinitely be substituted for each another so that they should never come to rest. "It is often said," Alain observes, "that experience alone can instruct us, but experience must be overcome and controlled."

—October 14, 1942

Fire, Water, and Dreams

The important contribution that Gaston Bachelard's recent books make to the study of artistic creation has perhaps still to be acknowledged by the educated reader. Bachelard's work has a philosophical significance to which books like *The Intuition of the Instant*, *The Experience of Space* and *The Philosophy of No*[1] have alerted readers in France and elsewhere. They represent a major attempt at assisting thought to become aware of the changes that new scientific thinking, that of Einstein, Planck, or Heisenberg, has in store for it. They provoke the mind by inducing in it a state of unease. They encourage it to discover itself in an aberrant or paradoxical guise. They seek to grasp it in its profound intervals, those moments of extreme deviation where its existence is a challenge to all traditional solutions. To the extent that it calls into question all the habits of psychology and turns to poets for revelations about thought, this work is of direct interest to criticism, which up to now, and with few exceptions, has remained attached to the most archaic concepts in both rhetoric and philosophy. The sudden entry of psychoanalysis into the criticism of the last twenty years was either inconclusive, or else remarkable more for its excesses than its discoveries. Gaston Bachelard reveals in his most recent works (*Water and Dreams, The Psychoanalysis of Fire*) what psychoanalysis stands to gain from refusing to be systematic, or to allow itself to be seen as a universal and incontrovertible solution to every problem.[2]

Criticism is generally interested in the formal imagination, which derives its resources from forms, colors, the picturesque, and words. In response to this approach, Gaston Bachelard began to study the material imagination, the imaginative forces that burrow deep down into what is primitive and eternal, claiming to capture direct images of matter, and behind what can be seen, to penetrate to the heart of substance itself, namely volume. It can be observed that certain sorts of matter instill in us a tendency to organize our dreams and to prolong them in the form of writing. If a reverie pursued with sufficient authenticity eventually takes on form as a poem, this is because it has its roots in something material, because it is fed by elemental images whose persistence and obsessive power determine the direction of the mind. It is even possible to distinguish between poetic souls according to the material elements from which they unconsciously draw their store of rapture. They depend in particular on a certain category of images, around which the deeper levels of the imagination gravitate; they are linked to a field of forces that, independent of all others, attracts their fears, their desires, and their impulses. There is a relation, says Bachelard, between the doctrine of the four elements and the doctrine of the four temperaments. People's imaginations are affected by fire, water, air, or earth, but each of them identifies with a single one of these primitive sites only, and only there does it find the forces that enliven it. "To uncover the secret of a true poet," he writes, "a poet who is faithful to his original language . . . one need say only one thing: Tell me your phantom of choice. Is it the gnome, the salamander, the sylph or the undine?"[3] These four fantastical creatures signify the four domains of reverie, the four points through which it must pass in order to achieve freedom.

If every artist has a preferred system of images, an enchantment to which he is unconsciously faithful, it is the task of the critic-alchemist to discover the regions where its sources are located. A study of two writers as close to each other as Edgar Allan Poe and E. T. A. Hoffmann reveals how external similarities are as nothing compared to the essential differences that arise because of their affinity with elements that differ radically from each other. Hoffmann is magnetically attracted to fire; he discovers in alcohol not only a stimulant for his genius, but also the substance that enriches it with images and provides his reverie with the admirable circuits along which it is constantly renewed. Edgar Allan Poe, on the contrary, is powerfully drawn to water: stagnant water, heavy water, water which in his imagination provides a material substratum for death, a home for calm and silent despair. The pond that belongs to the House of Usher, like the "dim lake of Auber" in the poem "Ulalume," are two symbolic figures taken from this inner geography. In them we recognize the horizon within which his dream encounters an invitation to die, the image of an everyday grave that is the receptacle for a nothingness distilled drop by drop by water as it flows. Alcohol for Hoffmann is a flame that is uplifted and terrified by its own phantasms. Alcohol for Poe is the water in which fire is extinguished, thus signifying death and oblivion.

When we recognize a complex of this nature, Bachelard observes, we appear in a better position to understand the unity and intention of certain poetic works. There can no longer be any question of accepting the rules of realism. For example, to read Poe's description of the Domain of Arnheim with the intention of reconstituting a realistic landscape from the details that match our memories would be frivolous and absurd. We should not evoke the real setting, but discover the fundamental element that underpinned the creative reverie and allowed it to develop as metaphor and as fiction. Freed from the realism that paralyzes them, these descriptions must be restored to their subjective function; they are a secret signal to us to descend beneath the surface of their manifest form, until we reach the hidden substance that provides the imagination with its dreams of uniformity, melancholy, and death. In the same way, the metaphors in which poetic truth declares itself in all of its audacity are not the result of transformations that have their starting point in realism, nor are they random inventions that signify only themselves; they are the signs of a deep-rooted system of coordination whose pattern can be reconstituted. Every true poet boasts his own metaphoric domain, and the ambiguities, discordances, and clashes of image to be found therein reveal, to the eye that goes in search of them, significant symmetries and an inner coherence where the true paths of reverie are revealed. By breaking open the forms of poetic expression, criticism can rediscover these paths. It descends into the obscure region of origin from where imagination, in a precisely determined fashion, derives its resources and its tendencies; it identifies the level at which imagination, thus magnified, henceforth obeys only itself, and escapes the gravitational pull of the forces that underlie it. There is indeed a moment in the creative endeavor when psychological as well as psychoanalytical description loses sight of its object. Having been part of the slow, monotonous life of an element, reverie finds freedom in the power of the mind, which remains the sovereign master of its goals. It goes beyond what nourishes it, and dies as it reaches fulfillment in the work that henceforth owes it nothing.

These theoretical views, which emerged in the course of his research into the objective conditions of reverie, are applied in an exemplary fashion by Gaston Bachelard, both in his study of a poet such as Lautréamont and his study of an element such as fire or water. If for instance we follow him as he analyzes images and works that are inspired by water, we discover what perspectives on the world of literature he offers to our gaze. The materializing imagination does not necessarily descend to the depths; it also plays across the surface of an element, and content with superficial and facile images, it lures us with charming falsehoods that provide common metaphors with their justification. Thence comes a poetry of clear water, of vernal water whose coolness expresses all of its reality. They are waters that can be seen and in which man too can see himself; Nausicaa bathes in them, and Narcissus sees himself in them; water is the true eye of earth; in eyes it is water that dreams. But soon these reveries deepen. Whereas on clear water the swan still symbolizes a desire for a licit beauty, for a nudity that is immaculate and free of suspicion, the poet who is driven by a more demanding imagination no longer sees in water a joyous source of fragmented, instantaneous images, but rather a support for images, a principle that founds, fascinates, and exceeds every image. We have observed how a writer like Poe makes contact unconsciously, through dull, silent water, with the matter that immortalizes his dreams. Water becomes the substance of substances, matter that is constantly in the process of dissolving and disappearing. Seen from another perspective, this is the same thinking as that of Heraclitus, who said mysteriously: "For it is death to souls to become water."[4] Gaston Bachelard gives the name "Ophelia complex" to the feelings that make us inclined to dream of a death that is without pride or vengeance, and the name "Charon complex" to the interminable dream which for all cultures links the thought of death to a journey on the waves. Wished for with Ophelia, accepted with Charon, our mortal fate is henceforth inseparable from the water that not only carries people away but also helps them to die completely. "O soul," says Christopher Marlowe's Faust, "be chang'd into little water-drops/And fall into the ocean—ne'er to be found."[5] And Paul Éluard: "I was like a boat sinking in enclosed water/ Like a dead man I had but one element."[6]

Other elements combine with this imaginary water to form more or less stable compounds, and so combined, they drive the imagination on to new adventures. There is the muddy paste made of earth and water with which *Homo faber* end-lessly experiments. There is the punch made from water and fire whose appeal Hoffman has shown us ("Water is a wet flame," says Novalis).[7] There is Poe's *Mare Tenebrarum*, a strange union of water and night, a substance in which dark-ness flows like matter.[8] Then water becomes a receptacle for maternal feelings ("The waters that are our mothers and that wish to take part in our sacrifices," says a Vedic hymn, "come to us along their own paths and give us their milk"). It is the symbol of a close, all-embracing, female presence (this is a dream of Novalis's, who in his sleep feels the sea pressing against him like a gentle breast). Finally, it is the image of purity, which purifies and protects and promises eternal youth like the Fountain of Youth, a maternal power that gives life in the midst of death itself.

Gaston Bachelard concludes his study with an analysis of violent water. The mind has a deep need to transform reality into a thing against which it can struggle in real combat. The world only appears real to it when it can grapple with it as an adversary. "I understand the world because I surprise it with my incisive force,"[9] and with an anger that it provokes and that responds to the provocation with a victorious conquest. Water is thus a hostile force that asks to be conquered as air, earth, and fire must be conquered. And just as it is possible to classify different types of imagination according to the ele-ments with which they are sympathetic, so too do the ele-ments make it possible to distinguish four types of anger and four types of victory that are particular configurations of vigor and of intellectual and poetic health. Thus Nietzsche is a walker who struggles against the wind. Walking is a form of combat for him; to the rhythm of his steps as they lead him nowhere, steps that respond to no sound and are necessitated by no journey's end, he advances until eventually he triumphs over the elements, in a victory that is endlessly renewed. Swinburne on the contrary is a swimmer, the hero of violent waters, for whom to leap into the sea is truly to leap into the unknown. He lets himself be rolled over and over by the sea, which he nonetheless masters, finding in this flagellation a secret pleasure. The Swinburne complex is marked by a virtual masochism, whereas the Xerxes complex, that of the man who imprints his dream of domination on the fury of the whipped-up sea, is clearly sadistic in inspiration.

Such images suggest to us what dreams continue to survive within old mythological forms. Bachelard is convinced that if such ancient symbols remain alive and effective through the rhetoric in which they are couched, it is because material imagination is always at work beneath the forms which make it manifest. Culture hands down words and forms to us, but true poets know how to awaken the original forces that lie beneath the conventional figures, and moved anew by the natural reverie that these figures once expressed, they transform them and bring them back to life. In that way, further metaphors are grafted onto existing ones, and the critic must descend to deeper levels in search of an interpretation of formal inventions that, from a realist point of view, are often unacceptable and absurd, but that regain all of their truth and their verisimilitude when linked to unconscious complexes. This conclusion presupposes notions that are drawn more or less directly from classical psychoanalysis. What is the value of such a claim? What does it mean? Is it not itself a sort of subterfuge that allows us to graft our own dreams onto literary works, rather than a way of bringing to light the true generative process behind a poem? *Water and Dreams* should be read as the work of an artist and a truly imaginative writer. Its analyses are brilliant and fine. They perpetuate the destiny of masterpieces. They endow them with new dimensions, abysses of horror or love, non-Archimedean spaces where imagination behaves according to singular laws. Moreover, not only are they persuasive but they are also true, to the extent that by making the fruits of the creative mind more mysterious, they associate truth with enigma.

—October 21, 1942

The Memory of Maupassant

Does the biographical study that Paul Morand has just devoted to Maupassant, soon to be followed by a critical essay, herald a return to Naturalism?[1] Is it a sign that Paul Morand, skilled as he is at anticipating public taste, has had an inkling that a vogue for an art without art is imminent, for an art that is somewhat crude if quite well crafted, and devoid of all creative rigor? Rather as he decided at just the right moment to take an interest in the subtleties of nocturnal impressionism, or the tormented vistas opened up by travel, or the fatuousness of the 1900s, is the aim of this thoroughly modern writer, whose way of grasping the significance of what is fashionable is not to submit to it but to shun it as soon as it becomes vulgar, to draw attention to a famous yet retiring writer as if he could be considered a likely guide for a certain type of literary youth? His skillful, balanced, and disdainful book is in fact far from offering unqualified praise, and rather takes the form of an elegant confrontation designed to divide two illustrious practitioners of the art of the short story and the novella rather than to unite them.

Maupassant's influence on the French novel was not very great and certainly not indispensable. The novel would have become just as vulgar and just as undemanding without the assistance of Maupassant. There were numerous substitutes who could also have led the novel genre down a road where it lost all authenticity and any connection with art. All Maupassant brought to it was success. He was not the leader of a school like Zola; he cared nothing for systems and manifestos; he was too uncultured to produce a theory of unculture, and too simple to write a defense of it. If he is the successor to Flaubert, it is only to the extent that he replaces willpower and tenacity with negligence and haste. He shows that the French story and French Naturalism can adjust to the absence of art and of any simple, robust spontaneity, just as easily as to the sort of pure art whose example and cult the author of *Salammbô* promoted. According to Albert Thibaudet, Maupassant is a model disciple, indeed the perfect disciple of Flaubert. That is true to the extent that the disciple reduces the art of the master to a set of tricks, and believes that this is proof that where invention and stylistic effort were once a requirement, natural artlessness and vigor without style are perfectly sufficient.

Maupassant's major novels are irredeemably banal and insignificant. Paul Morand gives robust short shrift to *Bel Ami*, for which Albert Thibaudet, who was curiously infatuated with the storyteller, had rather a soft spot. Everything is conventional and without rigor in these images of a society whose ridiculous features seem to be portrayed by an observer who is unaware of them. *Bel Ami* is not a type but a skillfully chosen name. *A Life* is less superficial. But *Strong as Death* is a book that can no more be called literature than those by Octave Feuillet or Eugène Sue. Its form is based on a type of ternary redundancy of the worst kind. The novelist always says three times what he wants to express without resorting to an image. For example, when an artist is afraid of getting older, his fear becomes "the fear that he had been emptied, had exhausted his subjects, had used up his inspiration"; when a high-society lady yields out of desire to someone she should resist out of duty, Maupassant writes three times: "She consented while resisting, she yielded even as she struggled, pressing him to her and crying: 'No, no, I will not!'" An artist does not just look at his drawings, "he leafs through the sketches, drawings, and rough drafts." And a bright sky is not content just to grow dimmer, "it softens, drapes itself sleepily over fabrics, and dies out amid thick curtains."

Maupassant's short stories undeniably display greater skill. They are swift and sometimes surprising. They reach their conclusion in a resolute movement that arouses and holds the attention. They owe almost nothing to analysis or psychology. They do not tell a story, in the way the realists understood story as a banal series of events. Their main quality, which is precisely the main interest of the short story, is that they convey a situation as it relates to the human condition, or to certain tendencies that a direct account could not convey. Paul Morand observes very shrewdly that this author who so lacks depth and is so incapable of poetry has a certain sense of the elemental forces in nature. He senses the material force of water, sea, and forest, the power that comes not from form but from matter, the original vigor that inspires myths and fascinates the imagination. The pleasure he finds in these forces is not that of a mediocre aesthete, who experiences them simply so as to describe them and describes them with complacency; he vaguely grasps their primitive reality, that lies in a density and plenitude whose images he cannot represent, but that touch him like forces that exist in an inexpressible dream:

> If my uneasy spirit sinks into a disdain for everything . . . my animal body luxuriates in all the intoxications of life. I feel something from every species of animal tremble inside me, all the instincts, all the obscure desires of inferior creatures. I love the earth as they do and not as you men do. . . . I love everything that lives, everything that thrives, everything that can be seen, with a love that is bestial and profound, wretched and sacred.

The situations whose significance is revealed in these tales often avoid being realistic because of what is extraordinary about their banality. Paul Morand says rather amusingly that the author of *Bel Ami* was blessed with an extraordinary gift of ordinariness. But that is true in another way. This Naturalist has a taste for what is improbable about what is natural, what is paradoxical about what is insignificant and what is extraordinary about what is ordinary. Many of his stories convey an impression of disturbing drollery, of a fiction whose lack of seriousness destroys life by rendering it derisory. A veritable farce is sometimes latent in them; but even in those tales where parody is absent there remains the seed of an obscure jest, the shadow of some cruel and comical image, which attempts to convey the vulgar side of life by secretly exposing it to laughter. Farce played an important role in the writer's life. It allowed him to express the unease with which he viewed things. It introduced an element of the fantastic into the world that was so real and so devoid of hidden depths to which he appeared to restrict himself. And furthermore, he needed to write a certain number of extraordinary tales in order to connect with the tangible things among which he came and went as an unconscious spectator. "The Hand," "Him?" "Solitude," "Diary of a Madman," "Horla," "Who Knows?"—all describe adventures in which life under the sway of strange powers reveals itself through horror, terror, and madness, becoming a state of distress that superficial reality cannot account for. The art is not always more refined or more authentic. But through the situations it expresses, it leads our attention down to a certain depth, and itself becomes more profound through the questions it requires us to ask.

Maupassant's madness has been the subject of countless studies. Paul Morand discusses it in his turn with great intelligence and tact. In one way, what seems to make the story pathetic is the fact that, however horrible it may be, it does not endow the author with one iota of tragic grandeur; neither legend nor dark symbol succeed in mitigating with their simulacra the crudeness of his vulgar talent; all we remember is the cheery man in a boat who, suddenly rich and glorying in his conquests, mindlessly disports himself at the "Grenouil-lère" with his chums; and what we do not see, beneath the rich, powerful, and famous man, is the latent lunatic, the victim of general paralysis observing his own deterioration and monitoring its relentless progress, while he hopelessly persists with the writer's task, in which he does not believe. In Maupassant's life and even in his tastes, all the features of an extraordinary existence are to found. This antiromantic is gripped by incurable ennui. "I am completely alone," he writes to Flaubert in July 1878, "because others bore me and I bore myself because I cannot work." And a month later, to Flaubert once again: "For three weeks I have tried to work every evening without being able to write a finished page. Nothing, nothing. So I am sinking gradually into black bouts of sadness and discouragement which I will find it very hard to get out of." To Countess Potocka in March 1884: "I am bored. I am bored uninterruptedly. I find everything tedious." And to another lady, Marie Bashkirtseff, in March 1884: "I haven't an iota of poetry in me, and I spend the best part of my time getting profoundly bored." This writer who is aware of how feeble his talents are ("I am incapable of truly loving my art, I cannot help feeling scorn for the thinking behind it, which is so weak, and for the form, which is so incomplete") has a preference for the forces of the night and the vagaries of the extraordinary. He loves the night: "I love the night passionately. . . . I love it with all my senses. . . . The day exhausts me, irritates me." He is addicted to drugs, ether, cocaine, morphine, and hashish: "I did not write a line of this book, which you will find so sensible," he writes, referring to *Pierre et Jean*, "without becoming high on ether; that drug gave me a higher lucidity, but it caused me much pain." And finally, the realist who was so attached to the precise outlines of life, to the observation of what is most common and most ordinary about mankind, lives surrounded by the most incredible apparitions, in a delirium that he inhabits naturally before eventually succumbing to it. If he speaks or says his name, it is as if he has a foreign word in his mouth. "I say my name out loud, several times in a row, then I no longer understand it at all—and finally, I spell out each syllable without understanding any better." If he looks at himself in the mirror, his image grows so dark that it becomes invisible. "In moments like that everything becomes confused in my mind, and I find it bizarre to see that head there, which I no longer recognize. And then it seems curious to be what I am, namely someone." And if he goes home, he finds it natural to see a man seated at his desk who is him, just as when he is seated at his table, he is unmoved when his double enters the room and dictates to him what he is in the process of writing. To Paul Bourget: "Every other time, when I go home, I see my double. I open my door, and I see myself sitting in my armchair. I know it is a hallucination at the very moment I am having it; is this odd? and if one did not have a bit of common sense, would one be afraid?"

Maupassant's madness produces episodes of somber brilliance over which the dark sun of Nerval and Baudelaire manifestly hangs. There is something fascinating about the trip to Lyon where, while he himself is apparently still in abundant health and intellectually in his prime, he accompanies his brother Hervé to an asylum. Hervé, believing himself to be in a quiet country house, leans out of the window in order to see the garden; two attendants grab him from behind and put him in a straitjacket, but as the poor wretch struggles helplessly, he cries out to his brother in a voice that tears a hole in time and vouchsafes the future: "Ah! Guy! you scoundrel! You are having me locked up! You're the one who is mad, do you hear me, you are the madman of the family." The day Maupassant himself can no longer control the outer signs of his delirium is no less extraordinary and solemn. It is January 1. So as not to worry his mother, and though he lives entirely surrounded by phantoms ("My mind is constantly wandering," he writes to Dr. Cazalis, "death is imminent and I am mad"), he travels to Nice to have lunch with her. But during the meal, his dementia intensifies, he starts to rave, and his mother, who has so far never suspected the truth, realizes with horror that her son is mad, mad like Hervé and perhaps like her. What a tragedy! Seeing his mother's distress, Maupassant realizes he has given himself away. He gets up at once, insists on taking his leave before his madness returns, and leaves the world of common sense behind for ever; then without a word, despite all the warnings and entreaties, he heads off in the direction of suicide and the appalling life of the asylum. He has left behind an account of his suffering in which his sense of decline is revealed in an extraordinary fashion. "If only I could speak," he wrote in 1890, "I would let everything out: all the unexplained, repressed and grievous thoughts I feel deep down inside me. . . . Thinking becomes a dreadful torture when the brain is nothing but a wound. I have so many bruises in my head that my thoughts cannot even move without making me want to cry out." And a little later, in 1891, he begins a deathly howling like that of a hunted animal: "The sort of dog that howls expresses my condition very well. It is a lamentable wailing that is addressed to nothing, goes nowhere, says nothing, and in the night utters that cry of fettered anguish that I wish I could let out. . . . If I could groan like them, I would go off sometimes, often, onto a great plain or into a deep wood and I would howl like that, for hours at a time, in the darkness."

If Maupassant's madness did not surround him with an aura of misfortune, it nevertheless gave luster to his talent by destining him for decadence; it laid bare the creative power he had within him through the slow destruction to which it exposed him; it revealed that he was not "a simple literary industrialist," as he himself claimed, by extracting from him these distressing cries on the subject of his last novel, *Angelus*, which he wrote without saying a word, in a total void: "I walk around in my book as I do in my room, it is my masterpiece," or else, "If this book isn't finished in three months I shall kill myself!" On several occasions Paul Morand identifies signs of

derangement in an art that appears robust and without ambiguities; in particular, he sees in Maupassant's liking for farce
a subsidiary aspect of his drama, a convulsive laughter that
anticipates his convulsive death throes; similarly, in his passion
for material elements—water, trees, forests—there is even
proof of a quite profound level of imagination on which, along
with the writer's dreams, the forces of unreason and nonsense
also drew. His biographer writes rather cruelly, "He gambled
on instinct and he lost. Through wanting man to be no more
than an animal he died on all fours, in a nursing home, bark-
ing and slavering." But from that instinct, which he preferred
above all for its crude vacuity, and that condemned him to a
living death, he probably also derived the only profound forces
that still give substance to his work, providing it with a sort of
frame without which it would be nothing, not even a memory.

—October 28, 1942

Unknown Romantics

The search for influences has always been one of the critic's pursuits, and although there are illusions that can impede it, it is a task that makes it possible to explain to oneself the interest one feels or does not feel for a given writer, the meaning one attributes to him, the angle from which one views him, and all those imponderable values that are obscurely bound up with literature. But if there is one thing that proves that the notion of influence or cause does no more than bathe the arts in an enigmatic light, it is the fact that it does not only work from past to future, from what precedes to what follows; it does not only elucidate today's writers by linking them to those of yesterday; it also uses contemporary art to cast light on the art of yesterday, as if the most recent works emitted a sort of radiance that is capable of imprinting and so converting into positive outlines the invisible forms of vanished literatures. Writers exert an influence over those who came before them, in the same way that they are subject to the actual influence of some of those who preceded them. They make the latter a little different to what they were, just as they in turn are, or appear, different by virtue of the models to which they can be compared. They are strange heavenly bodies that, rather than being visible the way certain stars are even after they have in fact become extinct, shed light on obscure bodies in the past that have long since vanished, and draw from them the finest and most enduring brilliance.

This phenomenon was perceptible during the twenty years that separate the two wars. That period saw a number of contemporary poets bring forth from the shadows, almost entirely thanks to their own brilliance, figures who came back to life as a result of their action, and became something one would never have imagined them previously to be. Abandoned hulls were transformed into proud ships ready for the long haul. Ruins rose again and became fine buildings. What was originally nothing proved capable of almost absolute reality and power. The result was a remarkable phantasmagoria. Naturally, it can always be argued that those exhumations merely reflected the vain and arbitrary desire of those who performed them to see themselves reflected in works that were known to no one. It could also be said that even if an operation of that sort was not totally contrived, it simply reflected the unpredictable but entirely explicable vagaries of posterity and fame. That is a perfectly reasonable view. But there are grounds for believing that the process can less easily be explained. It is as if, sometimes, certain writers could create or transform the works of the past by bringing them back to light once again.

Four of these figures who were once forgotten and now attract intense admiration form the subject of *The Birth of Contemporary Romanticism*, a recent book by Francis Dumont.[1] The selection is quite a judicious one. Two of these figures, Alphonse Rabbe and Xavier Forneret, have suddenly leapt from obscurity, and while still continuing to be unknown, they nevertheless shine mysteriously, like "stormheads" as André Breton called them.[2] The other two, Petrus Borel and Philothée O'Neddy, are less significant, but they have earned their place as contemporary icons. Francis Dumont tries hard to connect these writers with the idea of poetry made familiar by the Surrealist movement, which was particularly drawn to them. He does so with tact and integrity. It would have perhaps been better if his study had been less modest. It restricts itself to providing analyses that are too simple to shed any light on the works, and these are insufficiently commented upon to make one want to know them better. It remains singularly remote from the questions it encourages us to examine. And it does not always provide our imagination with the means to compose a portrait of these writers, who are real above all thanks to what is fictional about them, and who are not what they once were, but rather what they allow our reverie to make of them. The most interesting study is devoted to Xavier Forneret. We should be grateful to Francis Dumont for having assembled a number of documents relating to a life that was known about until now on the basis of only a few indications.

Petrus Borel and Philothée O'Neddy deserve their place in literary history. Both were part of the boisterous Young France group whose masters remain Théophile Gautier and Gérard de Nerval. Petrus Borel, who has never been forgotten, played the part of the rebel whose provocations served to frighten the enemy, and gave his friends their watchwords and their battle cries. In certain respects, these provocations could not have been more banal and superficial. They recall the prankish behavior of the Bohemians rather than any real contestatory fervor. They can be put down to youthful boisterousness, and merely give rise to fruitless commotion. Politically, Petrus Borel is a republican because he is against Louis-Philippe; in literature, he is a frenetic because he is against the bourgeoisie. All that is just passing fancy. However, this effervescence has a more serious cause, and one that certain literary movements will become acutely aware of a few years later. This spirit of outrage and scandal, expressing itself in a naïve fury, connects literature to something that goes beyond it. The members of Young France who call themselves Lycanthropes (wolfmen, halfway toward a twofold metamorphosis) claim to represent a total form of Romanticism. This does not mean that they are a little more Romantic than Lamartine or Victor Hugo, but that they already exist beyond Romanticism's limits, as a force that, in destroying everything it cannot tolerate, is nothing but a pure image of destruction. They aim to turn literature into the ultimate road to catastrophe, where not only bad literature and the bourgeois world will founder, but where literary reality in its entirety is also doomed to perish. Poetry calls itself into question and opens up a prodigious abyss for man, where everything becomes impossible for him, even poetry.

This is clearly the tendency that the Surrealists were very glad to rediscover in a set of writers who, in the case of most of their works, were hardly destined for greatness. With the exception of "Gottfried Wolfgang," which Francis Dumont, like Gérard Bauër, justly praises, Petrus Borel's tales concoct a bizarre hodgepodge out of the inventions of the fantastic and the horrible.[3] The vengeance of Andrea Vesalius, who dissects his wife's lovers one by one before laying her out on the dissecting table in her turn, seems like an unbelievable joke, and confronted with the misfortunes of Dina, who is raped, robbed, murdered by a boatman, and then thrown into the water, the very most we can manage is a laugh or a smile. But if we assume that these absurdities are aware of their own naivety and determined to turn themselves into an object of secret derision, they acquire new efficacy and new charm. The frenetic world that these two-bit crimes and fabricated follies inhabit not only takes the place of the real world where we think we live our uneventful lives; in the process of destroying that world, it also destroys itself, and having rendered the visible and the invisible equally suspect, it leads the eye beyond the ruins and the haunted castles toward a stranger, more unnerving land, toward something like nothing, which can only be conveyed to us through a sort of imageless dream. It is precisely to the extent that Petrus Borel's tales are utterly boring, and unbearable in literary terms, that they have attracted the attention of modern readers and offered them the key to a world lying beyond literature.

We have recently had occasion to mention Philothée O'Neddy (Théophile Dondey) when citing the amicable and indulgent pages that Valéry Larbaud devotes to him in his *French Domain*.[4] Though an undistinguished poet, he too has attracted attention because of the withdrawal that he imposed on himself prematurely; he asks too much of art, and in the end finds silence preferable to it; his was a minor act of literary suicide that posterity has fully endorsed. By contrast, the actual suicide of Alphonse Rabbe bestowed a dim, subdued, and yet glorious reputation on the strange figure whom André Breton called the last French moralist, and one of the greatest. *The Album of a Pessimist*, which Jules Marsan and Louis Andrieux allowed us to become better acquainted with about fifteen years ago, is illuminated throughout by the death for which Rabbe painstakingly prepared himself, which his writings hold up as an example and which alleviates what is ponderous and artificial about them.[5] What interests his modern admirers is the literary beyond with which his literature is enriched, thanks to the bloody end it anticipates; it is that partly double reading that incites us to decipher each page as if it were simultaneously the site of purely artistic values and a source of secrets that are totally alien to art; it is the act through which the writer suddenly transforms a literary work into a reality which no longer concerns literature. Alphonse Rabbe's suicide does not therefore display the usual characteristics of Romantic death. It is not only a spectacular challenge to life, a defense of melancholy and hopeless passion; above all it offers an example of that aspiration toward the impossible that characterizes the art of Lautréamont and Rimbaud, and leads it to renounce itself as art. Furthermore, his work is very far from being devoid of merit. Baudelaire read it and reread it; it revealed to him some of his most personal themes; it brought him intimately close to himself. We can even suppose that when Baudelaire considered committing suicide and set out in a (still unpublished) letter the reasons that moved him to do so, he was thinking of the "final letter" written by Rabbe ("all I have done is avail myself calmly and with dignity," he wrote, "of the privilege of deciding his own fate which every man receives from nature. That is all that I still find to interest me this side of the grave: it is beyond it that all my hopes lie, always assuming there are grounds for these"), and to be accompanied in this way by the shadow of a great poet is like the afterlife that Rabbe could only hope for in an uncertain future.

Xavier Forneret's case is more mysterious still. "He is perhaps the most extraordinary Romantic as well as the least well known," wrote Charles Monselet in an article for *Le Figaro* in 1859. And yet the life of the man they called the "Man in Black" or the Unknown Romantic does not seem to have given rise to any extraordinary events. Born in Beaune in 1810 and heir to a considerable fortune, dying in Beaune seventy-four years later almost a ruined man, he spent his life composing plays and books while trying to have them performed or published, and by the time he died, a complete unknown, amid the farrago of utter nonsense that he left behind there were a few pages of a quality that was both admirable and enchanting. The only trace left by the writer in the press of his time consists of an article by Jules Janin in the *Débats*, providing an account of the play entitled *Mother and Daughter* that is not too severe; the article by Monselet in the *Figaro* and a few articles in the newspapers that Forneret subsidized out of his own resources. His works seem to have been obliterated through indifference. They cast him into a veritable void, which was something he had an inkling of from very early on, though he did everything he could to overcome it. ("For the literary annals of the current part of the nineteenth century," he wrote when he was thirty, "there will be a book filled with an infinite number of names—excepting mine.") Why did he remain so totally unknown? That is a question asked by André Breton, who did not only do him justice but truly brought him to life. His eccentricities are no greater than those of the Lycanthropes. If rumor has it in Dijon that he lives in a Gothic tower and plays all night on a mysterious Stradivarius; if he has his books printed in large type, sometimes with just three lines to a page, and puts the word "after-end" after the word "end" (strange practices for which he does apologize), on the practical side he displays considerable stability, defending the ideas of his class in good bourgeois fashion and behaving like a solid man of means who unsuccessfully uses them to help himself emerge from obscurity.

Alongside the reasonable person whose ideas are often extremely banal, there seems to be a candid, clumsy being in him who is cast by the effort of literary creation into an unfamiliar world, where he becomes capable of the most mysterious formal inventions. His tales, poems, and maxims would be of no account were it not that images that are unusual and yet extraordinarily precise show them to be caught up in a reality that is shot through with strange visions. He has a naïve instinct for rare figures. He gives the impression of having spontaneously discovered metaphors that have multiple meanings. He combines candor with the complexity of picturesque figures. For example, in a description of a dream he writes, "A woman comes toward me; her heart is in her hand. All around her, a sword keeps emerging and withdrawing into the earth. It is as if this sword has ribbons on it and an eye that stares."[6] The naivety that, in a text that is mediocre or just plain silly, can suddenly bring to light an image that is extremely wise; the unpredictable inrush of light where nothing seemed destined to make it shine, are further evidence of his power to persuade and to dazzle. Here language truly opens up, and from within itself emits the inexplicable. Words that have hitherto reflected nothing are changed into refracted beams of light. There are no doubt only a few pages in which such gifts are completely in evidence. But "A Dream," "Diamond of Grass," "And the moon beamed and the dew fell," or "An eye between two eyes" are sufficient to reveal the value of Xavier

Forneret's curious poetic constitution, and to make him the model of those absurd failed creators whom we encounter now and then, lost in shadow that is veiled forever by the misfortune of initial neglect.[7]

—November 18, 1942

Refuges by Léon-Paul Fargue

"I am neither a philosopher nor a theologian nor a partisan. Perhaps I am only a poet because of the drama of seeing faces and facades die around me. I would like to be nothing but an overcoat thrown round my old soul, and with my gentle bag of tricks and my box of secrets, to trot through these apartments that are the big cities and the countries in which I have traveled." We must be careful not to let what writers think, let alone say about themselves, dictate what we think of them. Yet their confidences can be both subtle and profound. And when these come from one of those congenial spirits whom we cherish dearly, we accept them as pieces of that mirror in which those whom we for our part see in a less simple and even august light, naively reveal themselves as they would like to be seen.

Léon-Paul Fargue, from whose *Pedestrian in Paris* these lines are taken, occupies an irreplaceable role in French literature.[1] He represents literature not just as it is written, but also as it is lived. He peerlessly maintains age-old customs that would no longer exist without him, and that it would be tempting to disparage. He protects and ennobles a mode of conduct, a delight in conversation and a desire to be with others that for several centuries characterized the lives of many of our writers. Is what this vanishing tradition carries off with it more a matter of memories than of values? Let us not dwell on that. For as long as Léon-Paul Fargue, that finest of artists and sometimes secretive poet, perpetuates it in an age which is allowing it to die, that tradition will retain its charm and its nobility, and for the moment at least, elude the judge who seeks to condemn it.

In Léon-Paul Fargue there is an inner writer and an outer one. They are what he calls his "variables." The two books he has just published (*Refuges* and *Fast-Fading Pleasures*), are slight and rather too dependent on their original pretexts.[2] But they are charmingly written, and they will help deflect onto the outer writer the current of admiration one would have preferred to keep in reserve for the poet who is less easily approachable, who is concerned with what lies within words and who creates a landscape which is only visible to the inner eye. *Fast-Fading Pleasures* is a collection of articles in which we wander through the circumstances that make up the banality and the essence of everyday life, as if in a dream. *Refuges* is a "family album," a book of reminiscences from which the author with his personal life is almost absent, but which casts a favorable glow over what he loves, what is no more, and what thanks to him will exist for ever: the life of a Paris dedicated to goodwill and grace, the memory of a literary life inspired as much by futility as by scruple and success.

Léon-Paul Fargue is very clearly the inventor of a mythology where literature that is attached to things, houses, and people has become an emotional state that can be breathed and lived. And that state is both a subtle and a delicate one. From the cafés where he fosters it, from the ordinary yet strange Paris of memory, which emerges at night and fades with the day, there comes an indefinable reality, the soul in a form which the body finds congenial, something that is cordial without being vulgar, intimate without being familiar, something simultaneously open and undisclosed. What is thought and what is printed disappears temporarily behind what is said. And what is said, while having the importance of a fleeting invention, has meaning only as an echo of those deeper relations where we confide but reveal nothing, where we are on an equal footing both with others and with ourselves, and where what comes to light is neither friendship nor camaraderie, but rather a life that is conventional and perfect, a life that is a dream, a mist, mere pleasure and vain passion. This mythology has its chosen sites: Montparnasse, Montmartre, Saint-Germain-des Prés, as well as its customs and its odors. It is open to the world and impervious to nature. Shadows linger there, and there men become shadows. It is like a slumber full of whispers, which offers its dreams to insomnia and its refuges to the day's despair.

Latent in Léon-Paul Fargue's writing there has always been a defense of café life considered as the main adjunct of a flourishing literature worthy of the name. His latest books contain fragments of this. We go from the famous Mouton Blanc, frequented by La Fontaine, Boileau, Molière, and Racine, to the Procope, around whose tables Voltaire and Piron, then Diderot, d'Alembert, and Crébillon were to be found. All that is history and legend. But what interests a living person who has grown up with illustrious poets as his friends is to follow the erratic tracks of Verlaine at the Buffet Alsacien or the Rocher, to awaken the ghosts of Oscar Wilde and Ernest La Jeunesse at the Café Napolitain, or to revive the melodious life of Guillaume Apollinaire at the Café de Flore. What is the café? asks Fargue. It is the antidote to the salons, those arid temples to refinement where neither a bold idea nor a passion nor a mistress can enter. It is a place that is good for the soul, where pride is laid bare, where truth will out, and where even the most garrulous are expected to show discipline and restrict themselves to precise terms and robust images. The cradle of clubs and coteries, a school for cordial and boisterous sincerity and a source of battles and reveries, cafés have saved lonely

souls from perdition and brought some focus to the lives of
spirits accustomed to too much passion. They are a refuge for
brief lives.

Naturally, since these dusty, gray, and almost invisible loca-
tions provide landmarks for the mythical existence that is that
of literary reality, there is no way in which they can be seen
or touched. Imagination pursues them and memory preserves
them. They are out of this world, in a city that is real by virtue
of being imaginary, and present only when seen in the light
of the past. Léon-Paul Fargue's Paris is one of the best-known
inventions in contemporary literature. It is a rare combination
of simple feeling and singular image, of photographic landscapes and esoteric figures, a firm alliance between things that
are recognizable and phantoms that defy the eye completely.
Follow the streets through which the "pedestrian" guides us.
Everyone can find their past there. Everyone rediscovers the
stone, the face or the sky he once loved. But suddenly, unan-
nounced, the images become unhinged. Houses burst asunder
beneath a monstrous overgrowth of vegetation. A carnival that
is a mix of nightmare, solemnity, and irony conjures up hallu-
cinations and memories. Along riverbanks we hear fictitious
water lap with a sound of bells. We skirt round squares in
which night is amassing a fortune. We enter a ruined building
where, as if from down a tunnel, the voice of youth can be
heard, so deep and false and cherished. What is this city? Is it
the dream-child of some sleepwalking town planner? Is it the
town that history knew? Or is it tonight's invention? We lose
ourselves and reappear, as in a true myth where light and dark
are equally capable of showing us the way.

We come across these images during brief pages of prose
that, as the fancy takes him but also depending on their pretext, Léon-Paul Fargue angles either in the direction of the
poem illuminated by the demands of its obscurity, or toward
the facile and loquacious chronicle in which the least detail
relates to everything. These chronicles are the result of chance,
but from the genre in which they remotely have their origin,

the prose poem, they retain a dignity and a necessity that one is surprised to discover in them. Léon-Paul Fargue has made an effective contribution to the restoration of prose to its rightful place, after the vogue for free verse and a poetry freed from its obligations had threatened to break it apart. He feels very strongly that prose should never abandon its rules, and that it can only aspire to be a new voice for poetry by no longer trying to become poetic. Neither harmony nor rhythm, neither bold vocabulary nor syntactic invention are denied this language. There is no better example of prose than those texts of Henri Michaux's in which all the words are invented. But just as musicality in verse is in no way an imitation of the forms of music itself, so the harmony of prose is unique to it, and calls for means that do not alter its intrinsic nature. If need be, it is possible to invent a totally new language, the way Mallarmé did in response to intentions which he felt were betrayed by traditional forms: that is a matter of genius and pride. But prose itself has its architecture, its articulation and its movement, the only substitute for which is silence, and its laws, if we accept them, bring infinitely more than they allow if we merely oppose them. We should recall that Rimbaud with the *Illuminations* and Lautréamont with *Maldoror* established the dominion of the most authentic poetry over the most regular prose.

Metaphor is the great lever that Léon-Paul Fargue uses in order to bring everyday language up to the level of the successive forms that change it without destroying it. He needs the simple image as much as the unexpected figure. He scatters straightforward similes, picturesque comparisons, and curiously distorted thoughts in every direction. He creates monsters through allusion and wipes out the universe by misusing words. From expression to expression he constructs gigantic arches above which the unattainable passes on its way. It is of no concern to him whether he binds the unexpected to the all too familiar or the unusual to the habitual; his liking for correspondences means that anything whatsoever may randomly align itself with everything, and only partly seriously, he erects gaudy edifices that collapse in an instant. In this respect, his place lies naturally between the Symbolists and the modern schools who have made the search for image their overriding and privileged passion. "The vice called Surrealism," wrote Georges Hugnet, "is the unfettered, impassioned use of the drug we call image, or rather of the uncontrolled provocation of image itself, because of the unpredictable disturbances and metamorphoses that it brings about in the field of representation: for every image, every time, forces you to revise the entire Universe. And for every man there is an image which, were it found, would wipe out the Universe."[3]

It should be added, however, that if Léon-Paul Fargue occasionally uses metaphor to launch a veritable assault on the world, he often makes use of it in a less arrogant way, and the similes that clothe his text combine with each other like the shimmering items of a costume designed to amuse the eye. Their purpose is to cause pleasure rather than pave the way toward an essential myth that remains incomplete and locked in a perpetual struggle with language, as is sometimes the case with certain other writers. They are picturesque, external, and unexpected; they overlay each other without increasing; they repeat themselves by virtue of their very diversity, and if they eventually shatter the world of everyday perception, it is through their lack of seriousness, as if their gentle drollery condemned all these things to be demolished for being unstable enough to accept so many disguises. Read for example the charming virtuosity of pages such as "Aviaries" or "Aquarium" in *Fast-Fading Pleasures*: the mysterious birds and unknown fish strike up a resemblance with humankind that initially amuses the imagination, then lures it in disturbingly:

> One only has to venture among birds to become increasingly astonished. Only men and women could outdo certain species that Dream dreams up when it comes to refinement, ridiculousness or tragedy: fierce cormorants, bitter and in a scurry like one of Balzac's bailiffs, albatrosses with butcher's eyes, humpbacked, pot-bellied birds with

spoonbills and great tailors' doublets, ibises as red as lobster *rémoulade*, flamingos got up for a night on the town, and finally those giant penguins who for a thousand years have looked to me like botany teachers for distant princesses.

This is delightful and artful, but then, using the same means, it comes up against a mystery:

> Barn owls, brown owls, screech-owls and eagle owls are cathedrals of silence, roasted snowballs that glint like Gothic arches and which stare fixedly at cold embers shaped like viaducts on the incomprehensible horizon which they can only make out at night. I would like to caress them, touch with my hand these balls of false cruelty, scratch the head of these concierges for volcanoes, until I heard them purr with horror, suddenly, beneath the tender warmth of my careful fingers. But night birds are standoffish. They stick out their chests until they have made them into corbels, and turn their gaze of mystical surgery deep inside their unexplored Chinese vases.

Is Léon-Paul Fargue's art made solely, as he claims, out of the regret at seeing things die, and the wish to restore them to life through memory? Perhaps it is, because he does not close in on the impossible, he accepts the world as it was, he preserves its image by means of fond analogies. However, it must also be said of him that if he helps us hold on to this world by offering it an existence made from words, the equivalent of a reality drawn from figures and comparisons, he also fulfills another task, which is to transform it and incite it to undergo perilous metamorphoses, and eventually to drive it a little way towards the abyss. That is the danger of an art devoted to metaphor: it calls everything into question; but that is also its merit, and in the lament for the life of another era which Léon-Paul Fargue readily, too readily, intones, it is right that we should hear the wrong note, the unheard of note, which intrudes into it like the cracked echo of an enigma.

—December 2, 1942

Poetic Works

Among the new works of poetry that each day seems to bring, there are those that reveal the problems to which they relate almost transparently. They open directly onto poetry and are concerned with its essence. They are from the outset a reflection on poetry, on poetry considered in terms of its powers, expressed in myths that reveal its true complexion and heroically confronted as an absolute condition. As for the others, they deliver what they promise, without question and in a pure spirit of generosity, and are entirely given over to the charm of what can be discovered without enigma.

The little book which Paul Eluard has just published, *Involuntary Poetry and Intentional Poetry*, should be considered a truly poetic work, on a par with those other works in which words that he has chosen himself are presented with the portion of truth that he feels has been allotted to him.[1] But this book also has a theoretical purpose. It is in the form of a collection of texts taken entirely from other authors and grouped together under two headings, one allocated to involuntary poetry, the other reserved for intentional poetry. The term "involuntary poetry" applies, somewhat ambiguously, to texts that appear poetic to Paul Eluard even though their authors did not intend them to be so, or that are poetic in a different way from what those authors intended, or that seek to be poetic even though no artistic intention lies behind them. Intentional poetry places the stamp of consciousness on literary fragments that basically are exactly what they should be.

The purpose of this slim volume takes us back to the era when Lautréamont's slogan "Poetry should be written by everyone, not by one person" and William Blake's maxim "All men are alike . . . in the Poetic Genius" were used to denounce what it was about poetry that could allow it to become the expression of a conscious, personal art. These debates may appear futile and anachronistic. But after all, why should that be so? Even if many poets no longer feel the urge to linger over these questions, and if their poems reject them like the debris or playthings of a bygone age, as questions they nevertheless retain their authenticity, since they continue to attract and to challenge a poet as alive, and as much in the forefront of young poetic minds as Paul Éluard is. . . .[2]

The collection of poems which Pierre Emmanuel has just published with the title *Orphics* illustrates the drama that condemns the poet to use words, take pleasure in them, and even find in them a sort of ecstasy, while in reality he is venturing into extreme regions where words are at risk of breaking apart in a voiceless spin.[3] Pierre Emmanuel possesses an extraordinary faith in the powers of language that expresses itself both in the form of his poetry and in its persistent choice of themes. For him, poetry remains linked to language; it calls words forth in sequences governed by an oratorical rhythm; it arranges them in vast groups without purging them of their prosaic intent; it places its trust in them while expecting from them, just as they exist, in prose formed into sentences and constructed according to an expressive syntax, the same purity of effect that the Symbolists sought from combinations of new words. Although its formal invention is sometimes brilliant,

and its images composed with no concern for immediate intel-
ligibility, its unstinting nature, its imperious abundance, and
its generosity with words are what give Emmanuel's poetry its
character. It is language that rules it; it abandons itself to the
impulsiveness of language and is governed by a desire to be
everything. Whereas poets who find inspiration in symbolic
art seem to use language only reluctantly, allowing it a role
merely as a concession and seemingly by accident, the poems
of *Orphics* grant it exclusive dominion, and in the midst of its
impurities and its uneven harmonies join with it as if it were
a spring that could only fully quench the thirst by becoming
a cataract or a torrent. Similarly, the Orpheus theme, whose
every angle is tirelessly explored by Pierre Emmanuel, constantly brings him back to this primacy given to language.
Orpheus is the man who introduced language into the Under-
world, who would not admit defeat in the face of the inexpressible, who subjugated fear of death through his rhythmic
incantations. In itself, that was a tragic victory. It is not possible to exercise supreme authority in language without expiat-
ing it. The poet who has given a name to forbidden things,
replaced silence with the word silence and soothed the deepest
levels of human care through the magic power of the word,
will inevitably be torn apart in the end by a myriad passions
born of language.

> . . . O thirst
> for vengeance that turns Orpheus against himself
> and raises out of hatred for the man he was the army
> of furies born of him, and women by their bellies
> but horrible and mutilated without his love,
> who search in his body for the intact mold, the still warm form
> where they can take on flesh! The soul groans
> beneath fingers that undo duration strand by strand.[4]

Conversely, in the collection he has published with the title
Terraqueous, Guillevic's poetry is suspicious of words that are
too ponderous and recoils at the rhetoric of avalanche and

profusion.[5] His brief, enigmatic poems single out objects or
elements whose disturbing reality is adequately conveyed with
a few brushstrokes; the mystery of things does not come from
their "soul," from the bias [*parti pris*][6] they adopt or from the
life they are assumed to have, but from their elemental interior, from the meaning of their material nature.

> Was it absolutely necessary to make such a fuss
> About a chair?
> —It isn't involved in the crime.
> It's old wood,
> Resting,
> Forgetting the tree—
> And its rancor
> Is powerless.
> It wants nothing more,
> It owes nothing more,
> It has its own giddy whirl,
> It is self-sufficient.

Rhyme is lacking in Guillevic's[7] verse, and there is no
attempt to create an immediately perceptible harmony. But
every word has its place in a unity where silence is a counterweight to everything, and calculation, dream, and friendship
conjure up a dense and schematic world, which is more real
than the living one.

Claude Roy's art as it appears in *The Childhood of Art* is
both ingenuous and self-aware, with a grace that is quite
unspoiled by a charming desire to please.[8] It takes pleasure in
the offerings that the world provides, and naturally couples
the gentlest and simplest of language with the emotion they
provide. His words espouse that emotion freely, providing an
echo of themselves, following on from each other verse after
verse and tracing out an inner design that adds a supplemen-
tary dimension to meanings that are always clear. One is
tempted to hold them up to the light and look through them
to see what visible calligrammes appear when innocence comes

into contact with irony and melancholy, and is lured by them
into a state of exquisite refinement.

> It's simplicity itself to love you for ever
> All you need do is surrender to the waves.
> This shoulder for me is the sea and the day
> and the tranquil beach where the flocks graze
> the great flocks of the day that slumber at night
> when from the horns of the cattle the birds fly off
> bats of silk owl osprey screech owl
> and the people of the dark along the slow waters . . .
> It's simplicity itself to wait till very late
> for the gentle, awkward flood of shadows without houses
> living among its dead it's simplicity itself
> to love you always as the seasons flow by.

If in order to picture this mix of refinement and candor, in
order the better to hear this voice artfully singing of its
naivety, those who like comparisons may well seek out paral-
lels with Guillaume Apollinaire, it is again the author of the
"Song of the Ill-Loved" who comes to mind when Maurice
Fombeure mixes the rhythms and techniques of popular
poetry with virtuoso feats of language in *On Bird-Back.*[9] There
is something felicitous about this guileless combination. It
requires the ease that is to be found in songs and roundelays,
where movement is more important than words. But the
images here are less spontaneous, and a preference for natural
things sits alongside a love of illusion and a taste for artificial
décor:

> My Lord of Framboisy
> feeds
> His unicorn dry bread
> And herrings hung on the wall
> But the unicorn wants
> To be fed on fresh bread
> It refuses to eat
> And that puts its life in danger.

There would seem little point in trying to identify a common direction to all these poetical works. The revision of values that poetry tends to carry out in every poet is still far from complete, and indeed it would be absurd for it to be so. No one can reasonably expect works by Audiberti, Ganzo, La Tour du Pin, Armand Robin, Lanzo del Vasto, or Pierre Emmanuel to establish a tradition that could set them against or distinguish them as a group from their immediate predecessors. The observations that have been made on this subject over the last few months are the product of futile preoccupations, and they reflect either a clumsy desire to see things clearly, or an infantile need to associate poetry with contemporary events.

—December 9, 1942

Bad Thoughts by Paul Valéry

The books that Paul Valéry has brought out over the past few years resemble each other by the disorder of their composition and their disdain for any meaningful organization. All of them are notebooks, more or less, containing in fragmentary form either essays or brief reflections, which are the forms his thought adopts when it wishes to display its incompleteness and the spontaneity of its exercise. They are only books by chance. The occasion that produced them suggests that it could also destroy them. Like many others, they hang by a thread—that of the stitching that holds them together; but like only a very few, they also seek not to hide the fragile manner in which they are put together, and they make no bones about the fact that they are not what they are.

From the first *Varieties*,[1] which appeared twenty or so years ago, to the *Bad Thoughts and Not So Bad*,[2] which have been available only for a few days, the bother of having to write books that can be deemed to provide their own pretext has become more and more apparent, and goes hand in hand with a literary activity which has not always been conspicuous by its absence. Those *Varieties* were made up of essays that were sometimes substantial, fully developed and firmly structured, and that, as little books in their own right, could easily do without the larger book in which they accidently found themselves. But the works that followed—*Analects, Rhumbs*, and *Things Kept Quiet*,[3] among others—were content to be assembled from fragments that could in no case pass for works in miniature. Taken from the "log book" in which Paul Valéry has kept a tally of his thinking since his youth, they are free of any concern for order or volume. They are brief rejoinders that momentarily interrupt the silence of purely internal reflections. In them, the mind appears in the lightning-flash that separates it from itself. What is nascent, changing, and fleeting seeks an entry into consciousness, where it shines just as it is, rectified just enough so as to keep up an appearance of incompletion.

Nothing about this aloofness from coordination and completion in a written work should surprise us. Paul Valéry has always insisted that what he likes about work is simply work, and he has let it be known that only some external intervention or circumstance can persuade him to interrupt its movement and turn it into a fixed state. A book thus appears to him as no more than a random interruption of the flow of reflection, and he does not approach its composition as an authentic problem whose solution should take precedence over other more decisive problems. In this respect, he seems willing to sacrifice form to content, on the pretext that the indefinite capacity for renewal that characterizes the mind can hardly adjust itself successfully to the vague convention represented by the structure of a book. A poem is a strict set of formal requirements to which language responds to the best of its ability, because such compliance also brings to thought a renewed transformative power. But the form of a book has less exciting virtues; it is tempting to go on seeing it as an untoward episode, an untimely conclusion in which the will of another, be it the reader or the publisher, substitutes itself for that of the author, who would prefer never to have to bring things to an end. If this attitude bears a curious resemblance to that of Mallarmé, it is also quite distinct from it. Mallarmé, too, could never put the finishing touch to his poems, and he pursued the ideal of a fundamental book of which his public output was merely the shadow or the disdained by-product. The works that he did allow to appear were merely the product of chance, compared to that essential work where every random element should have been abolished by the dice-throw. But whereas this endless quest expressed a desperate concern for poetic perfection considered as higher even than the highest value (since it represented them all in their purity), the same quest in Paul Valéry's case reflects a degree of indifference toward the intrinsic value of literature, and a very obvious preference for thought and its exercise. In short, the perfection to be found in his works is merely an accident. It is not what is wished for, but merely the movement that brings it about. Similarly, art as a result deserves infinitely less attention than the means it presupposes. Mallarmé's mind worked with absolute rigor toward the poem he wished to produce. Paul Valéry's mind works with equal rigor toward to the labor whose effect is the poem.

There are perhaps other reasons for the way these books appear, born as they are of persistent discontinuity and systematic hiatuses. This refusal of a certain type of discursive logic is inseparable from the order inherent in such a way of thinking. If the pieces of a literary nature in Paul Valéry's work bear the mark of the coherence which is required by the laws governing their development, those texts whose inspiration is more intellectual, including the *Introduction to the Method of Leonardo da Vinci*[4] itself, avoid wherever possible having to organize themselves too precisely along the lines of any analytical or dialectical order. Or more exactly, those texts begin by sticking quite closely to a methodical form of development; they assert, they prove, they progress perfectly predictably. But there almost always comes a moment when this quiet, confident way of proceeding appears to weigh heavy on the mind that is directing it; whereupon that mind stops and veers off; it detaches itself from its demonstration and turns back toward itself; it sets aside the object to which it had been attentive and pays attention only to that attention; it flees what it was in order to reflect on what it could have been. Possibilities are what attract it, and though it does not lose sight of the subject on which it was originally focused, it ceases to deal with it methodically and connects it to a greater number of mental elements than the initial project would seem to call for. This preference for combinations and transformations is stronger than the wish to dispense with them in order to reach a clear result. The mind is all the more willing to abandon its goal, for believing that it can also reach that goal by watching itself approach it and practicing at getting there, and for believing also that this is basically the sole outcome that its procedures require.

If Paul Valéry abhors all systems, this is therefore not only because of the dogmatic claims from which they are inseparable; it also comes from the specific movement of his thought, which does not always lead to a result, and in place of a specific arrangement of elements designed to achieve a goal, prefers to bring into play an indeterminate number of possibilities relating to that goal. Hence his increasing indifference toward any sort of demonstrative writing in which reason combines with something other than itself. Aphorisms, turns of phrase, observations, remarks in which the mind appears and then fades, incidents in the life of the mind, episodes on the margins of a forever hidden drama, responses to a language that remains obstinately unspoken—the assembling of all these "details" gives the mind an image of what is "essential" that is more faithful than any provided by those arguments where it is sacrificed to what it wishes to say. Here, contradictions prove nothing; repetitions are not a sign of negligent monotony; and silence, as a gap between sentences that is also their bond, has a rigor that excludes it from the sphere of things that are vague and impure. The reader is not invited to dream about what is not said; he finds no mystery in this void that interrupts him and throws him back on himself.

These *Bad Thoughts*, collected in the same order as that of the letters of the alphabet, which also sometimes determine their key words, initially convey little more than the infinite variety of subject and method that characterizes their development. Paul Valéry's manifold curiosity is to be found there, as well has his verbal habits, the "whys" with which he undermines a self-satisfied idea, the answers that are merely hidden questions, the series of self-evident statements that culminate in an enigma, the metamorphoses of the easy into the difficult, the complex into the simple or the same into the same. Just as perceptible as in almost all his other works, there is that passion of the mind for itself, which makes it prefer the experience of the life of the mind and the mastery of its operations over all certainty, all fixed relations between two ideas. On one side the dislikes, the interrogation of the values that are generated in mankind by its suffering and its fears, its hopes and its torments, or by what is vague, be it a word that is not clarified or an idea not reduced to its own terms, an emotion masquerading as a theorem, the unwarranted transfer of one order into another, an assertion designed to outlive the conditions that gave rise to it; but on the other, what happens in the course of every usage, belief, or dogma, the intellect and what it is when it functions and contrives, "our own way of working, which alone can teach us something about everything," the act of thought considered as indifferent to the content of thought, the universe of possibilities, the infinite connections offered by language. These themes are present or assumed even in the trivial reflections that appear to disregard them. "I," says every remark on every subject, and finding itself everywhere and not content to be anywhere, this "I" imposes its presence and its absence on anything at all, then discusses it simply in order to be.

However, in these thoughts, which are so faithful to what they were intended to be, some movement can be discerned that distinguishes them occasionally from those to be found in other collections. They are "bad" thoughts because they disrupt the usual order, but also because more than others, they make room for chance, disorder, or the irrational, room for that "evil" that restricts the possibilities of the mind. Paul Valéry's works are sometimes drawn toward the forces of the powerful mind, which, surrendering to its finest moment and thinking with its own forms, employs its resources to the full, turns itself into a homogeneous, joined-up whole and does not just make discoveries but adds to those discoveries. At other times, they consider the obstacles that prevent thought from ever being entirely thought: the intemperance of a human nature fertile in fallacies, excuses, and pretexts, what is weak even about pride, the random aspects of intellectual life and last of all the sense of indifference and futility with which, having attempted everything it was capable of, intellectual passion discredits and sacrifices itself. Depending on the role they give to each of these two movements, Paul Valéry's works take on the appearance of being good or "bad." In fact, only his first works, at least those that first confronted him with the problems he has never turned away from, give almost unalloyed expression to the confidence of the mind in its own means and the superb joy it derives from its own virtuosity. The others are less interested in these inner labors; they yield more to the irrational display of passion with which humanity gives itself the impression that it thinks, whereas it is in fact just an urge to live; they put into the past tense once and for all the celebrated sentence from *Variety*: "I was twenty years old and I believed in the power of thought."

It should also be said, however, that such touches of disillusion, or rather this sort of self-abandonment, do not result from the difficulties that mental activity encounters in its search for a clear, precise awareness of what it is. It is not because the world, or reality, confronts the desire for identity, order and precision in which intelligence finds expression with its own fundamental peculiarities, that the mind stops believing in itself; the mind does not claim to understand nature, it claims merely to discover, in its effort to understand, the enactment of its own laws, and to take pleasure in the art with which it strives against what is difficult to know. It derives its victory from its failure, since it constantly exists thanks to the struggle in which it is defeated but not undone: "The world continues; and life, and the mind, because of the resistance that things that are difficult to know exert against us." In some respects the values in which, from his youth, Paul Valéry enshrined the solemn significance of his existence remain unassailable. They are his alone, but they are immune to any threat. They are based on assumptions which he put forward arbitrarily, but in total agreement with himself; all other values, those which he calls vague and intangible Things and which are linked to human anguish and emotion, he has discarded as having neither importance nor significance for him. He has vested all possibility in the mind; in the mind and not in knowledge, in the mind attached to the passion of its exercise and not to its results. He could therefore only be deprived of all reason for living, were humanity suddenly to lose its mind, and were the object to which he has devoted all his curiosity and all his powers to disappear in a catastrophe that would no longer allow it even to appear possible.

The mind cannot stop believing in itself as long as it is concerned for itself, and this is all the more true perhaps when it does not know than when it does. But it can acquire a sort of inattentiveness to the unique problem posed by the way it multiplies out into its own virtualities. It loses interest in itself, it yawns over its activities, it says with M. Teste: "Tired of being right, of doing what succeeds, of the effectiveness of my methods, must try something else." Trying something else consists in condemning one's rigor and reverting to an amused contemplation of the world with which one has to do simply because one has to try and live. Disenchantment is now not characterized by the condemnation directed at what is impure and mediocre, but by one's curiosity about it and the charm it provides. One finds pleasure in something other than one's own problems, and one yields to it as if finding enjoyment in self-denial. Paul Valéry wrote one day: "I am much less of a puritan than I would have liked to be. Circumstance has caused, and increasingly causes, this puritan to melt and slacken." The "bad thoughts" come from that puritan who, though suppressed, still endures, and seeing the indulgence of the mind for so many of the objects in which it tries to lose itself brilliantly rather than discover itself, proclaims to it, beneath the refinements of language, all the ennui he derives from the pleasure of being in the world.

—December 16, 1942

New Novels

Here we have four novels that in fact are tales. These distinctions—tale, novella, novel—always appear rather naïve. Does it make much sense to introduce clear divisions into what remains chaotic when seen as a whole? What separates a novel from a tale may appear clear and precise to us, but it is much harder to see what a tale is and what a novel is. Roughly speaking, a tale possesses a technical simplicity that is lacking in other works of fiction. It does without diversity of either theme or point of view. If it is not a pure story, it often submits to an abstract intention that is only half-concealed by the twists and turns of the narrative. It proves or demonstrates something. In Voltaire's *Candide*, an undisguised theoretical intention that we are quite happy to discern is allowed to show through in its descriptions and its scenes. The novel, on the contrary, uses its temporality to conceal what it reveals through the clarity of its episodes.

Georges Magnane's new book *The Strong Men* is a depiction of sporting activity.[1] The two main characters are sportsmen, and the plot takes us to an eight-hundred-meter race, two boat races, some all-in wrestling training, and a ski run down a steep slope. The way these events are described is so precise and natural that they become a distraction from the actual story in which they occur. With this book, Georges Magnane proves himself to be one those very rare writers who can talk about sport without ever overdoing things. He does not turn it into an occasion for lyricism the way Montherlant does, or a make it a pretext for learned commentary in the style of Jean Prévost, or a theme providing perfect images as in Giraudoux. He says what he has seen and experienced, and literature simply offers him an opportunity for rigorous language. It is quite remarkable that a writer should be ready to talk about sport with sincerity and accuracy as if it were a normal activity, without that mix of artifice and caution that distorts its true nature.

Sport provides the main theme of the book, but the sporting scenes do not give the impression of being there in order to justify the story itself. It is for that reason too that they are natural. The story of the "strong men" is that of a fellow whose face, unequaled vigor, and athletic talent do not convey exactly what he is. He appears primed for a tragic life, but he is vain, self-obsessed, and ultimately rather cowardly. He constantly deceives those who admire him, and also the person he loves. It is not an easy task to unmask men who are totally different from what they appear. The subject takes shape only very slowly. What is simple remains concealed. There is plenty of time to admire the descriptions of boat training on cool spring mornings, the accounts of races where hopes for victory are dashed, or the rough-and-ready stratagems of a body that lives in the immediate, does not dream, and soberly organizes its effects. And when the plot reveals where it is going and the rather heavy-handed outcome it has in store, our interest in it lies with what has made it possible to write a book that is more important in its details than when seen as a whole, and so natural in some of its scenes that the story in which they take their place appears justified as a result.

The Wind Is Rising by Marius Grout is a work that confirms
the keen interest that his first book aroused when it appeared
last year.[2] In *Advent Music*[3] he depicts a curious, vaguely mystical man who seeks to arouse a sense of the miraculous in his
compatriots by means of a series of naïve and simple actions.
This agent of the marvelous fails, but his failure makes him
aware of his true vocation, and having gone blind and become
a poor, wretched, abandoned soul, he appears to his village as
someone laden with privilege, and so without realizing it, fulfills the mission he believes he has been entrusted with. *The
Wind Is Rising* consists of a twofold variation on the same
theme. A schoolteacher whom his pupils do not respect and
whose family neglects him falls in love with a girl to whom he
is giving private lessons. He thinks the time has come for him
to live. He becomes impassioned, surpasses himself, and wins
the respect of his family and his class. But all this is vain
endeavor. He does not have the strength to seize hold of the
light he has glimpsed. He is ruined by scandal. The shadow
for which he was destined finally reclaims him; he is content
to have failed in life, to have been just a rough draft that fades,
having achieved nothing. In the same town, a young curate
experiences a similar temptation. He is energetic and uncompromising. He wants to reform everything. He is full of apos-
tolic zeal. But having been given the task of organizing study
groups for young people, he meets a girl whose spiritual
beauty attracts him, and one day he realizes that they love each
other. Will he draw back? Will he say no? He is persuaded
that he must undergo this ordeal, that he must find God not
by remaining beneath the horizon of life, but by going beyond
it. He must be what he is destined to be; otherwise, his spiritual existence would no longer have any meaning. An old doctor who has witnessed both of these adventures points out
their common significance. Two human beings wanted to live.
They could feel the wind rising. But one of them lacked
strength, while the other, too much a prey to his strength,
tried to possess the light without knowledge of it. Is that what

it means to experience life? "Our most solid experiences," replies the doctor in conclusion, "the only living ones, those we are nourished by and with which one day we may nourish others, and which will justify us, I believe, in the eyes of God, are those experiences that our flesh has never known."

Marius Grout's book has exceptional qualities. It is written harmoniously and soberly. The destinies that it evokes play themselves out between sun and shadow, and they are like thoughts that seem to take the form of veiled realities. From their abstract origin they retain a sort of profound absence. They are what they are, but they could be different too. Solitude keeps watch over the forms that the story gives them, as does the unquiet imagination of their author, who is reluctant to abandon them and would like to take them back and have them to himself. It is clear that Grout's book is more of a tale than a novel. The purpose that directs it is clearly apparent beneath the fictions that overlie it. The hand that guides it is quite perceptible. M. Rousseau's diary and that of Father Courbertin are combined only so as to bring about the conclusion, and this conclusion, which is proposed by the old doctor in the form of a letter, is the moral in relation to which the two stories were written. These stories have the speed of development, the unvarying light, and the indifference to duration that are found in the tale. From the beginning, the teacher is headed for catastrophe; the priest suddenly changes character, and from being an uncouth apostle he becomes an indulgent being led astray by passion. Why? We know or guess why, but there is no time to get used to this sudden event. The outcome looms; what the story is designed to show matters more than the story itself.

Perhaps the difference between the novel and the tale comes from the meaning that is added overtly to the tale and that, in a novel, cannot be considered separately. The meaning of a novel, even a symbolic one, is its fiction; this does not presuppose a meaning that lies beyond it; it is entirely expressed through what it is; story, characters, events, form, and content are the inseparable ingredients whose combination in the work was necessary for it to mean something. The meaning of *Ulysses* lies in every detail, every scene, and all of the verbal invention that reflects the fertility of its main theme. As with a poem, it is impossible to grasp that meaning outside of the words and the formal detail into which the author has translated it. There is something anomalous about wanting to sum up the meaning of a novel in a few abstract sentences, when in reality the novelist needed the entire concrete expanse and all the calculated diversity of his book in order to reveal that meaning. A tale can sometimes become unbalanced if the message it bears, through being visible behind the plot, distracts attention from the plot or makes it appear unnecessary. What we understand so clearly at the end of a tale tries to take its place and be all that remains in our memory.

The Wind Is Rising is itself somewhat distorted by being mirrored too clearly in what gives it its soul. This soul becomes detached, becomes all that is visible and the novel itself is no more than the silt left behind once what is purest has been extracted. Nevertheless, a sort of secret life remains attached to these characters whose mystery appears to be exhausted. This is because their author is present alongside them; the "I" through which they express themselves is the projection of a deeper self that is revealed as they gradually confide in each other; the problems that sum up their actions are identical to the burning questions that have arisen in an individual life. What is weak and inchoate about the teacher, what is impetuous about the young curate are as it were two faces of the same soul, which can sometimes tolerate only shadow, and at others desires light so intensely that it extinguishes it as soon as it obtains it. The impression given of a profound experience that we know only fragmentarily is what ultimately gives Marius Grout's book its true character. The story calls out to its author and, with the reply that the latter decides to offer, enriches the voices of characters that are otherwise too abstract.

In Maurice Toesca's book *Clement* the traditional features of the tale are no longer concealed.[4] There is open interplay between allegory and story, and each event is presented to the reader as an enigma for which he must find a meaning. What makes the search an agreeable one is the fact it takes place amid a chaos of incidents, boldly linked together by a sometimes engaging and sometimes laborious fantasy. To penetrate the absurd only to encounter a commonplace is not without its charm. The Clement in question, a victim of his own innocence, embarks on a burlesque sea journey during which he loses his friends but finds morality. He lands on an island where the men have blue skin and the women lay eggs; he becomes delirious; he prophesies; he declares, "Only solitude guarantees freedom; only freedom guarantees power; the only power is power over oneself, the only freedom, freedom in relation to oneself." For *Clement* is an essay on freedom. This is not a problem for the reader. He even enjoys observing the way the author plays with him, sometimes in order to hide what he means and sometimes in order to make it clear. He feels he is dealing with an intelligence that, like the cuttlefish, covers its retreat with an inky cloud; and though the game may appear to him rather pointless, he accepts it because of the apt turns of phrase to which it occasionally gives rise.

Finally, with *If the Sky Falls*, Roger de Lafforest offers us an allegorical tale containing neither mystery nor camouflage.[5] The reader is entertained. It is a sort of dialogue of the dead, and it makes liberal use of the opportunity to judge this world that is provided by the invention of another. The beyond is merely the comical reverse of earthly existence. The dead man becomes aware of the mediocre person he was during his lifetime, but he persists under another guise with the mediocrity that is the fate of all humanity. In this realm where pagan fictions are linked to the trappings of a more modern beyond, it is the same plots, the same passions and the same weaknesses that drive the dead into a state of perpetual motion. Zeus, who is invisible though vulnerable, is merely a head of state who governs as economically as possible, allowing plots while avoiding revolutions. Professor Pessimas's pastime is reforming creation. Yankos is a lawyer who organizes public health groups. Where is the true world, where the old one? Here below at least, death puts an end to what is a ridiculous adventure; but after death, escape is no longer possible, and we have to put up forever with the absurd friends and the miserable self that fate has given us as companions. Roger de Lafforest graciously accepts the prejudices of the genre he has chosen. He takes pleasure in their simplicity. He does not conceal their effects beneath the illusions of an obscure story. Everything in his narrative is precise, clear, free of folly and nightmares. The tale dallies with death and leads us through the shadow without offering us even the shadow of a truth.

It is clear that the monotony of their method, the way time is elided in them, their sobriety of tone and above all the theoretical nature of their main theme lend each of these four works the appearance of a tale or long novella which appears and disappears beneath the outer shape of a novel. Georges Magnane was unable to prevent his novel from appearing almost nothing alongside the sporting descriptions he filled it with; the story he tells does not command our attention; it remains empty; it fades away. In the same way, in Toesca and de Lafforest there is, so to speak, an absence of soul that renders futile the intellectual exercise whose threads they have carefully woven together. The mind retains only their intention, and in itself it appears rather insignificant; what use is a book if its art is not made inseparable from thought by the style with which it marks it? There are more secrets in Marius Grout's story, and it is this ponderousness, this solemn silence, this indiscernible something extra that, in spite of all the explanations that the author has seen fit to give us, adhere to his work like a truth that cannot be spoken, and prevent it from turning to nothing once the reader has discovered its conclusion.

—December 23, 1942

From Taine to M. de Pesquidoux

Saint-René Taillandier's book about her uncle, Hippolyte Taine, has many charming qualities.[1] She recalls her childhood memories with considerable ease and sensitivity, as if the shadow of an illustrious name did not hang heavy over them. She is careful to avoid bringing the pure, ethereal impressions she recalls from her earliest years into line with what earnest formality would require. As a child then as a girl, she remains entirely herself alongside the philosopher whom we remember as the inimitable model of a particular sort of severity and gloom. In the convent of Saint-Germain where she spent her youth, she would sometimes hear the nuns saying to each other: "The Chevrillon girl is M. Taine's niece." But the words "M. Taine's niece" remained impenetrable to her. Was she meant, in the name of the person in question, to display more knowledge and wisdom than was usual among ordinary children? Or did the members of this religious house wonder what sort of thoughts a young mind had been exposed to by living alongside a man so aloof from all religion? One day, the chaplain quizzed her on the history of the church, but without

success. He was puzzled by this; he wondered if such ignorance was the norm in the Taine family. The knowledge and
the errors of this little girl thus appeared to him as reflections
of immense learning and mysterious leanings, for which she
was made to bear the responsibility in all innocence.

Saint-René Taillandier is very cautious when she talks about
her uncle's life. Her book is made up of highly personal memories, yet it avoids anything that might appear incompatible
with discretion. It is by no means certain that Taine's life contained any great secrets. The interior probably always corresponded to the exterior. There are none of those monsters that
lurk intimately, we suspect, in certain writers, and make them
very different from their works. But although it is very likely
that he had nothing to hide, he also insisted on the fact that
he had nothing to reveal as if this were an inalienable right,
and the most innocent attempts at making public some of the
circumstances of his private life were more unbearable to him
than any insult. Saint-René Taillandier recounts how the wife
of one of his friends saw fit to publish a short article full of
admiration and sympathy on the subject of Boringe, Taine's
estate, and its guests. "I would have preferred it," said Taine,
"if she had gone off with the silver." Throughout his life he
never allowed his photograph to be published, and he rejected
the most tentative overtures of modern publicity with icy
politeness. And yet as we know, he had high ambitions for his
mind. As Albert Thibaudet put it, the morning bell at the rue
d'Ulm said to him and his companions at the École Normale
what Saint-Simon's servant had orders to say to his master
every morning: "Get up, Milord, you have great things to
achieve." Success meant nothing to him. But he did not shun
it, and even courted it, because everything that drew attention
to him ensured a wider audience for his ideas. Hence in order
to obtain a prize from the Academy, he had no hesitation
about writing a eulogy to Livy, even though he did not think
much of him. "There is no place for vanity," he said in 1850,
"my sole aim is to acquire notoriety."

Utterly entranced by the memory of her youth, Saint-René Taillandier's goal is to leave behind a more genial image of her uncle than the one that his books have led us to imagine. To his niece he never appeared professorial or doctrinaire, and she is always saddened when she recalls the remark of one visitor: he looks like a puny cross-eyed professor. She persuasively evokes a serene, amiable, intimate, and radiant presence, scarcely distracted by the authority granted to his work and by his reputation for severity. We have the proof that Taine laughed, indeed laughed out loud, on reading an appeal from a local counselor to his minister: "Trade and industry reach out to you, M. le Ministre, with arms they do not have"; or when he had read to him amusing stories signed with the unusual pseudonym "Merino Sheep." There is evidence too of his genial and kindly attitude towards children. He loved their jollity and would share in its power of rapturous harmony even though its general validity left him unconvinced. He would look at his daughter and say "she is the early spring," "she is Hebe"; his niece was Miss Maud, and he would ask Miss Maud the question, "What do you think of life?" and smile when she gave the reply he anticipated: "I find life delightful, uncle."

Saint-René Taillandier seems to regret the veil of gloom and sadness that the pessimistic philosophy of her uncle cast over his face. She defends him against this pessimism as if it were an unhealthy state of mind, and she refuses him the right to be gloomy until, after 1870, he was able to verify the infinitely remote causes of his country's woes in his great history. "The more he ventured, or rather sank into this history," she writes, "the sadder he became." On the other hand, she spends a long time giving a very convincing account of Taine's calm, that stoical disposition which provides intelligence and conduct with a guarantee of rectitude, freedom, and order. When he was just twenty, in a most moving correspondence with the young Prévost-Paradol he could write: "If I have enough strength to persevere with this ambition—to be of service to other men through the profession I embark on—I shall obtain what constitutes good health for a person: that is to say calm. Calm, do you fully understand what it is? It is the supreme good!" On days when his niece is suffering the pangs of a deeply troubled soul, he advises her to write a life of Pope Honorius. And when later he is accused of being ambitious and eager for popularity he remarks, "There is no better sedative [*calmant*] than extreme contempt." Saint-René Taillandier gives us an image of this calm, which, while perhaps mythical, is nevertheless rather fine. The philosopher of *On Intelligence* (1869) occasionally went swimming in the lake with small children. On such days, lying on his back as if suspended between heaven and earth and with his eyes closed, floating motionlessly in a sort of slumber that turned him in on himself, his face was a solemn mask whose extraordinary nature awakened strange thoughts, even in little girls. He was entirely reduced to being a head, resembling that of a dead man in its august rigidity and yet content with a peace that meant nothing to it. We may imagine that this self-abandon in what remained rigor, this certainty adrift on the water, this seriousness cut off from all communication in the bliss of a perfect swim, were a reflection of the calm on which Taine had based his life. He rested there while remaining oblivious of everything, like a man who does not go soft when in repose, but on the contrary, by ceasing to be, becomes solemnly himself.

The correspondence of the young Taine, one of the most remarkable in the nineteenth century, seems to reveal that this calm was not only a defensive reaction on the part of a highly strung sensibility, nor a simple precaution in order better to apply scientific method to human affairs. "One ought not to parade one's feelings on paper; no sobbing, no shouting, even if this means being taken for a curt, impassive automaton." This exhortation is already the product of Taine's experience late in life, and it definitely does not take account of all the inner developments to which the enquiries of a mind confidently opposed to itself had exposed him from his early youth.

As we know, he burned the more personal notebooks in which, at the École Normale and in preceding years, he wrote only for himself, and these confidences were no doubt unlikely to reveal any extraordinary flights of the soul; but in one or two of his letters one senses the determination of a man who, like Hegel, experienced a dull anguish in the face of knowledge, feared he would founder under its weight and who, so as not to confine the meaning of existence to it alone, entrusted his intellectual life once and for all to a rigorous and precise discipline. It is to that resolve that Nietzsche is no doubt referring when he writes in his eulogy of Taine: "A resolute man, bold even in despair, whose courage and energy were not crushed by the fatalistic pressure of knowledge." Later, it is the futility of knowledge when it is vainly made accessible to men, the difficult art of living, and those bitter fruits of life: restlessness, affliction, and misconduct, which made him experience calm as the only way to remain in harmony with himself. Saint-René Taillandier tells of how, having found her uncle weary and sad one morning, she asked him what was causing his listlessness; the reason was that the previous evening, until very late, he had been leafing through an atlas and had then been unable to sleep after looking at all the traces of a troubled universe, swept along by an eternal movement and constantly reduced to its own folly. Taine's calm corresponds to this image of a historian who cannot peruse an atlas without being deprived of sleep. He sees people pointlessly embarking on great wars, pointlessly unleashing revolutions and pointlessly sacrificing what they are to what they wish they were. He remains calm, but he can no longer sleep.

It would not be difficult to find in the work of Joseph de Pesquidoux numerous features that render it amenable to Taine's theories. Perhaps there is even a real unity of spirit and intention between the two writers; each of them likes small details, observing them, describing them, and never judging them to be insignificant or unrelated to what is to be demonstrated; each of them derives an ideology or an ethic from what they analyze; in the name of what they have seen, they prescribe for mankind a reminder of those conditions that can best allow it to sustain and organize life; they seek to bring man as close as possible to himself; they express him in terms of what makes him stable, tranquil, and concerned for tradition. In Taine's case, as we know, ideology was the first thing to cease to interest him. Even the great themes of his history have endured only as conventions that fed his mind, gave it strength, and urged it on towards a moment of supreme intelligence and literary power. And what survives is the beauty of his great portraits, the deep color of his ideas, the development of his language and the violent passion that binds him to the study of France's destiny, the way a flame is bound to the wood that it causes to glow. With Pesquidoux the lessons are simpler; they consist of a glorification of custom and an emphasis on natural disciplines; they coincide with the traditional conclusions that can be drawn from our history; they will no doubt endure for as long as does that side of man that needs to be reassured and saved from itself. But however significant they may be, we may legitimately refuse to make the literary work that expresses them also depend on them entirely, and we may consider this work solely in terms of its aesthetic value, free of all the services it may render.

The book that, with the title *French Soil*, brings together the best pages from *Our Home*, *On the Glebe*, and *The Book of Reason*, reveals very effectively some of the qualities that make Joseph de Pesquidoux an exceptional and demanding writer, and one who is very different from those with whom it might be tempting to confuse him.[2] The short chapters devoted to the acts of sowing, plowing, and planting vines, to haymaking, coppicing, and the threshing machine, reveal the surprising literary value of minute and methodical description that is devoid of anything picturesque and almost cold. This way of making available to our gaze, in every detail, the objects and actions that we thought we knew, and that even seemed so familiar to us that we took them to be yardsticks for everyday life, momentarily makes our images change course and reveals to us a reality that is not surprising, that we know, yet that is nevertheless quite new and seems to have metamorphosed into itself. No extraordinary figures are required for the writer to transform what is into what is. He refrains from subjecting things to the distortions of an artistic gaze; on the contrary he outlines them with ever-greater precision; he captures them with common words and brings them close to us thanks to the objectivity of a vision from which our prejudices are absent. This power of estrangement provided by the imitation of a perfectly humble and usual reality is one that painters know well. It is less common in the literary arts. Anecdote, the resources of invention and the search for unusual effects all generally prove unavoidable for anyone who writes, and who thinks of himself as a realist while remaining totally unaware of the constant untruth of his realism. Only descriptions of "entirely invented objects" that are interminable thanks to their minuteness and care, such as those to be found in Raymond Roussel's work, can succeed in giving us the same impression of dream, rigor, and enchantment as that provided by painstaking depictions of landscapes or "entirely familiar objects." What matters is not whether the object is initially familiar to us or not; it is the hallucinatory character of an analysis that seems unable to come to an end.

The scenes taken from *Our Home* or *The Book of Reason* are free of contrivances. Individuals put in few appearances. We see the sower, the ploughman, or the harvester as if each of their activities required us to consider humanity as a whole, and not the features that separate one individual from another. The stories exclude everything that could make them true for one person only. They have a classical generality and they depict for the future, as well as for today, the Armagnac peasant who needs no distinct characteristics in order to be distinguished and who, like man himself, is an individual by virtue of what is most general about him. Among the stories that leave some room for anecdote, it is agreeable to recall that of old Sarruilles, the silent, authoritarian, all-powerful peasant who with age silently sheds each one of his privileges and from season to season abandons the plow, hands the responsibility for sowing over to someone else, withdraws from his yards, and finally, bowed by age, refuses to eat at the common table and has his meals served to him separately by his eldest son on a salt tub he made himself. This image of a man who stands down from his duties with as much pride as Charles V, and willingly reverts to being a servant because he cannot go on being a master, leaves a powerful impression on the mind. Joseph de Pesquidoux's style gives him dignity and a sort of stable truth. It makes us momentarily the equals of this ingenuousness rich in secrets, which we realize has greater value than many a more learned symbol.

—December 30, 1942

Notes

INTRODUCTION BY MICHAEL HOLLAND

1. See "Introduction" by Michael Holland in Maurice Blanchot, *Into Disaster: Chronicles of Intellectual Life*, trans. Michael Holland (New York: Fordham University Press, 2013).

2. See Annette Wieviorka and Michel Laffitte, *A l'intérieur du camp de Drancy* [Inside the Drancy Camp] (Paris: Perrin, 2012).

3. "Situation de Lamartine," *Journal des Débats*, 22 July 1942, 4; "Lamartine's Position," in *Faux pas*, trans. Charlotte Mandell (Stanford, Calif.: Stanford University Press, 2001), 152–55. Henceforth *FP*.

4. "La Terreur dans les lettres," *Journal des Débats*, 21 October, 1941, 3; "Terror in Literature," *Into Disaster*.

5. In *La NRF des années noires. Juin 1940–juin 1941. Des intellectuels à la dérive* (Paris: Gallimard, 1992), Pierre Hebey observes: "When we think of the day-to-day life of those men of letters we can only feel extreme unease. What did they feel every day when confronted with situations and actions that we might have thought would offend and outrage them? These questions come thick and fast, and for the most part go unanswered" (20).

6. Maulnier was a contributor to *L'Action française* throughout the Occupation and remained close to the Vichy regime. However,

in a series of articles entitled "The Future of France" that appeared in 1941, he resolutely rejected the idea that a national revolution in France could be imposed from without by a foreign power, and argued that French humanism could not countenance racist dogma, since the French do not constitute a race. See "L'Avenir de la France, I–V," *La Revue universelle*, January–June 1941; see also *La France, la guerre et la paix* (Lyon: Lardanchet, 1942), 185 ff. Though events would eventually expose the criminal absurdity of such a position (which was also that of Maurras), there were those who defended it and remained men of honor.

7. Blanchot claimed that his "participation in 'Jeune France' took place at the beginning of 1941"; see "For Friendship" (1996), in Maurice Blanchot, *Political Writings, 1953–1993*, trans. Zakir Paul (New York: Fordham University Press, 2009), 136. However, he was involved with Xavier de Lignac in a final attempt to transform the movement before it was finally dissolved by Vichy in July 1942. The fullest available account of the "Jeune France" experiment is to be found in Michel Bergès, *Vichy contre Mounier* (Paris: Economica, 1997), 23–169. See also Christophe Bident, *Maurice Blanchot. Partenaire invisible* (Seyssel: Champ Vallon, 1998), 158–66. Further detail is provided by Philippe Nord in "Pierre Schaeffer and Jeune France: Cultural Politics in the Vichy Years," *French Historical Studies* 30, no. 4 (Fall 2007): 684–709.

8. Blanchot gives a detailed account of this venture in "For Friendship," 135–36. Again however, what he says is misleading as far as dates are concerned. As with "Jeune France," he claims that the *NRF* episode happened at the beginning of 1941. However, several accounts propose a chronology that stretches from December 1941 until mid-1942. See Alban Cerisier, *Une histoire de la NRF* (Paris: Gallimard, 2009), 438–44, and (for a more reliable account) Christophe Bident, *Maurice Blanchot. Partenaire invisible*, 216–18.

9. Maurice Blanchot, *Aminadab* (Paris: Gallimard, 1942); trans. Jeff Fort (Lincoln and London: University of Nebraska Press, 2002).

10. Maurice Blanchot, *Comment la littérature est-elle possible?* (Paris: Corti, 1942); "How Is Literature Possible?" trans. Michael Syrotinski, in *The Blanchot Reader*, ed. Michael Holland (Oxford: Blackwell, 1995), 49–60.

11. Maurice Blanchot, "For Friendship," 134.

12. See "The Silence of the Writers," *Into Disaster*.

13. "In Search of Tradition," *Into Disaster*.

14. See Blanchot, "Unknown Romantics," in this volume, 170.

15. "The only way to impose silence on too noisy a world would have been to pay heed to one or two inner voices drawn from as close as possible to their original time." "Chronicle of Intellectual Life," *Into Disaster*.

16. The quotations in this paragraph are from "Considerations on the Hero," in this volume.

17. In "Thirteen Forms of a Novel," *Journal des Débats*, 26 May 1943, and *A World in Ruins: Chronicles of Intellectual Life*, 3 (forthcoming), Blanchot refers to Brasillach without naming him in order to dismiss his literary activity out of hand: "a few years ago there was a novel that set out to use every known novelistic technique; over seven chapters, the plot was organized and varied using seven different techniques. These antics have not left any trace in the history of the novel." The work by Brasillach is *The Seven Colors* (Les sept couleurs) (Paris: Grasset, 1939), a paean to fascism and Nazism.

18. "On Insolence Considered as One of the Fine Arts," *Journal des Débats*, 6 January 1942; *FP*, 306–10. This text gave rise to what remains the most serious polemic ever generated by the question of Blanchot's political past. See Jeffrey Mehlman, "Blanchot at *Combat*," in *Legacies: Of Anti-Semitism in France* (Minneapolis: University of Minnesota Press, 1983), 6–22.

19. See "From the Middle Ages to Symbolism," this volume.

20. Both the reference to Montherlant's readiness to contest everything and the (unfavorable) comparison to Nietzsche in "A User's Guide to Montherlant" (this volume) no doubt reflect Blanchot's discussions with Georges Bataille at this time.

21. The struggle between Drieu and Paulhan came down to whether Montherlant was or was not part of the editorial committee of the review (Claudel and then Valéry both refused to accept his presence). See Alban Cerisier, *Un histoire de la NRF*, 443–44; Christophe Bident, *Maurice Blanchot. Partenaire invisible*, 217–18.

22. As well as the two articles from 1941, see "The Writer and the Public [L'écrivain et le public]" (November 1941), *Into Disaster*; "Montherlant's Play [Sur la pièce de Montherlant]," *Journal des Débats*, 31 March 1943, 3, and *A World in Ruins: Chronicles of Intellectual Life*, 4 (forthcoming); "Nobody's Son [Fils de personne]," *Journal des Débats*, 10 August 1944, 3, and *Death Now: Chronicles of Intellectual Life*, 4 (forthcoming).

23. See "Chronicle of Intellectual Life" (on *The Harvest of 1940*), 4 May 1941; and *Into Disaster* and "Considerations on the Hero," this volume. See also Jacques Benoist-Méchin, *Éclaircissements sur Mein Kampf* (Paris: Albin Michel, 1939, 1941).

24. There are three articles on Jouhandeau: "Chaminadour," *Journal des Débats*, 4–5 August 1941, 3, and part of "Chaminadour," *FP*, 227–33; "De l'oeuvre de Jouhandeau [A Work by Jouhandeau]," *Journal des Débats*, 19 May 1943, 3, and *A World in Ruins: Chronicles of Intellectual Life* (forthcoming); "Le 'Je' littéraire [The Literary 'I']," *Journal des Débats*, 1 June 1944, 3, and *Death Now: Chronicles of Intellectual Life* (forthcoming). On Chardonne, see "The Novel and Morality," *FP*, 234–38, and on Fraigneau, "Tales and Stories," this volume.

25. See "Mediterranean Inspirations," *Into Disaster*.

26. See the letter from Blanchot to Roger Laporte dated 22 December 1984, which is incorporated in Jean-Luc Nancy, *Maurice Blanchot. Passion politique* (Paris: Galilée, 2011), 61. For a later instance of this, see Maurice Blanchot, "A Letter," trans. Leslie Hill, in *Maurice Blanchot: The Demand of Writing*, ed. Carolyn Bailey Gill (London: Routledge, 1996), 209. The letter is dated 24 December 1992. "Conversion" is also the term that Jeffrey Mehlman uses to describe the way Blanchot changed during the war. See "Pour Sainte-Beuve: Maurice Blanchot, 10 March 1942," in *Maurice Blanchot: The Demand of Writing*, 227.

27. On this count I find I must take issue with Christophe Bident's otherwise fine and subtle presentation of this phase in Blanchot's career. For the best possible motives, Bident shows that he is ill at ease with his subject's willingness to publish in the *Débats*, and feels a need both to underestimate the significance of the "Chronicles" in their entirety, and to present the *Débats* in a uniformly negative light. See *Maurice Blanchot. Partenaire invisible*, 181–99 and 218–23.

28. "If it can be said that I was in the wrong/at fault [*S'il y a eu faute de ma part*]" (*Maurice Blanchot. Passion politique*, 61). "Une faute" in French can mean either an error or a fault, but also a sin.

29. Further details of Guy Herpin's career can be found at http://brutus.boyer.free.fr/chroniques/g_herpin.html.

30. "L'insecte ennemi de l'homme," *Journal des Débats*, 6 January 1942, p. 3, signed G.M.

31. "A propos du doryphore," *Journal des Débats*, 15 January 1942, 3, signed Hachon. The letter is printed just above Blanchot's article on Drieu la Rochelle, "From the Middle Ages to Symbolism" (this volume).

32. See *Into Disaster*.

33. "Défense des lieux communs," *Journal des Débats*, 25 October 1941, 3.

34. "La solitude de Péguy," *Journal des Débats*, 30 June–1 July 1941, 3; "The Solitude of Péguy," *FP*, 279–82.

35. "Au jour le jour. Les deux solitudes," *Journal des Débats*, 6 July 1941, 1.

36. In response to the often vicious polemic that followed Bergson's death in 1941, his wife decided to make public the following statement from her husband's will: "My reflections have brought me closer and closer to Catholicism, which I see the as the fullest expression of Judaism. I would have converted, had I not seen the gradual build up over the years of a dreadful tide of anti-Semitism that is about to engulf the world." Quoted in Floris Delattre, "Les dernières années de Bergson" (Bergson's Last Years), *Revue philosophique de la France et de l'étranger* 3–8 (May–August 1941): 136. See also http://etoilejaune-anniversaire.blogspot.fr/2011/12/louise-neuburger-veuve-de-bergson.html.

37. For a brief biography of Mario Meunier see http://forezhistoire.free.fr/mario-meunier.html.

38. See www.persee.fr/web/revues/home/prescript/article/bec_0373-6237_1975_num_133_2_460072.

39. For an obituary of Jean Mousset, who died in 1946, see www.persee.fr/web/revues/home/prescript/article/polit_0032-342x_1946_num_11_3_5795. Mousset wrote a long and highly positive review of Blanchot's *Thomas l'obscur* over two pages in the *Débats* of 30 October 1941, 1–2.

40. Mario Meunier, "*Dante* par Dmitri Merezhkovsky," *Journal des Débats*, 10 October 1942, 3. For Blanchot's article, see this volume. Curiously, in a reversal of the situation, Blanchot will review authors already written about by Meunier on four occasions in 1942: Pierre Brisson's *Molière* on 10 June (Meunier reviewed it on 10 May); Daniel-Rops's *Psichari* on 9 September (Meunier, 4 July); Léon-Paul Fargues's *Refuges* on 2 December (Meunier, 7 November); and Saint-René Taillandier's *Taine* on 30 December (Meunier, 12–13 December).

41. Jean Mousset, "Portrait d'un héros," *Journal des Débats*, 12–13 September 1942, 1; "Guynemer" [unsigned editorial], *Journal des Débats*, 12 September 1941, 1.

42. Maurice Blanchot, "Considérations sur le héros." See "Considerations on the Hero," this volume.

43. See Jeffrey Mehlman, "Pour Sainte-Beuve," 214–15.

44. Ibid., 212–13.

45. John Erskine, "Be Fair to France," *Collier's Weekly*, 13 December 1941, 18. Accessible at http://www.unz.org/Pub/Colliers-1941dec13-00018.

46. In 1940, Pierre Bernus published *Le dossier de l'agression allemande* (Paris: Payot, 1940), which pulled no punches in its denunciation of German militarism: "The spectacle offered by Hitler and his collaborators is one of the most appalling there has even been in all history" (7). For a brief account of Bernus's career, see www.persee.fr/web/revues/home/prescript/article/bec_0373-6237_1952_num_110_1_460271.

47. See "The Politics of Saint-Beuve." This level of speculation allows at least for the hypothesis that the decision to publish the first of Blanchot's chronicles devoted to Paulhan's *Fleur de Tarbes*, "Terror in Literature," on October 21, several weeks before the other two, might not be unrelated to the fact that the previous day, a member of the Resistance shot dead a German officer in Nantes.

FROM THE MIDDLE AGES TO SYMBOLISM

1. Pierre Drieu la Rochelle, *Notes pour comprendre le siècle* (Paris: Gallimard, 1941).

A NOVEL BY COLETTE

1. Colette, *Julie de Carneilhan* (Paris: Fayard, 1941); in *Chance Acquaintances* and *Julie de Carneilhan*, trans. Patrick Leigh Fermor (London: Secker & Warburg, 1952).

2. Virginia Woolf, "Modern Fiction," in *The Common Reader* (London: Hogarth Press, 1925), 16.

3. Ibid., 18.

BERGSON AND SYMBOLISM

1. Only the beginning of Blanchot's original article is included here. The rest provides a complete chapter of *Faux pas* with the same title.

2. Emeric Fiser, *Le symbole littéraire* (Paris: José Corti, 1941).

3. André Rolland de Renéville, *L'expérience poétique* (Paris: Gallimard, 1938).

TALES AND STORIES

1. Jean Giraudoux, *Littérature* (Paris: Grasset, 1941). Blanchot's review of this work appeared in the *Débats* on January 20, 1942. It is included in *Faux pas*, 91–95, under the title "Literature."

2. André Fraigneau, *L'irrésistible* (Paris: Gallimard, 1935); *Camp volant* (Paris: Gallimard, 1937); *La fleur de l'âge* (Paris: Gallimard, 1942).

3. André Fraigneau, *La grâce humaine* (Paris: Gallimard, 1938).

4. Robert Francis, *Histoire sainte* (Paris: Gallimard, 1941).

5. Thomas Mann, *Die Geschichten Jaakobs* (Berlin: S. Fischer Verlag, 1933), translated by H. T. Lowe-Porter as *The Tales of Jacob* (London: Martin Secker, 1934), then by John E. Woods as *The Stories of Jacob* in *Joseph and His Brothers* (London: Everyman's Library, 2005). The French translation to which Blanchot is referring is by Louise Servicen, *Histoire de Jacob* (Paris: Gallimard, 1935).

THE POLITICS OF SAINTE-BEUVE

1. This article is the second one not to appear under the heading "Chronicle of Intellectual Life." It begins on the front page of the paper and continues onto the second. Blanchot refers to Maxime Leroy, *La pensée de Sainte-Beuve* (Paris: Gallimard, 1940), and *La politique de Sainte-Beuve* (Paris: Gallimard, 1942).

2. André Rousseaux, *Le monde classique* (Paris: Albin Michel, 1941).

3. Henri Brémond, *Roman et histoire d'une conversion* (Paris: Plon, 1925).

4. Victor Giraud, *Port-Royal de Sainte-Beuve* (Paris: Mellottée, 1929), 49.

STORIES OF CHILDHOOD

   1. Marc Bernard, *Pareils à des enfants* (Paris: Gallimard, 1942). The book received the 1942 Prix Goncourt.

   2. Odette Joyeux, *Agathe de Nieul-l'Espoir* (Paris: Gallimard, 1941); Jean Cocteau, *Les enfants terribles* (Paris: Grasset, 1929); *The Children of the Game*, trans. Rosamund Lehmann (London: Harvill, 1955).

JEAN GIONO'S DESTINY

   1. Jean Giono, *Triomphe de la vie* (Paris: Grasset, 1942). Jean Giono, *Les vraies richesses* (Paris: Grasset, 1936).

   2. Jean Giono, *Que ma joie demeure* (Paris: Grasset, 1936); *The Joy of Man's Desiring*, trans. Katherine Allen Clarke (London: Routledge & Kegan Paul, 1949).

THE REVELATION OF DANTE

   1. Dmitry Merezhkovsky, *Dante*, trans. Jean Chuzeville (Paris: Albin Michel, 1940).

THREE NOVELS

   1. Luc Dietrich, *L'apprentissage de la ville* (Paris: Denoël, 1942).

   2. Julien Blanc, *L'admission* (Paris: Albin Michel, 1941); Elizabeth Porquerol, *Solitudes viriles* (Paris: Albin Michel, 1942).

AFTER *DANGEROUS LIAISONS*

   1. Jean Blanzat, *Orage du matin* (Paris: Grasset, 1942).

   2. Jean Giraudoux, "Laclos," in Choderlos de Laclos, *Les Liaisons dangereuses* (Paris: Stendhal et Compagnie, 1932), 8–15.

THE MISFORTUNES OF DURANTY

   1. Edmond Duranty, *Le malheur d'Henriette Gérard*. Préface de Jean Paulhan (Paris: Gallimard, 1942). The novel originally appeared in 1864.

2. Edmond Duranty, *La cause du Beau Guillaume* (Paris: Editions Colbert, 1942). The novel originally appeared in 1867.

REALISM'S CHANCES

1. Louis Guilloux, *Le pain des rêves* (Paris: Gallimard, 1942); for Marc Bernard see "Stories of Childhood," this volume.
2. Jean Follain, *Canisy* (Paris: Gallimard, 1942).
3. Jacques Robert, *Invitation à la vie* (Paris: Albin Michel, 1942).

JUPITER, MARS, QUIRINUS

1. Georges Dumézil, *Jupiter, Mars, Quirinus* (Paris: Gallimard, 1941).

IN THE LAND OF MAGIC

1. Henri Michaux, *Au pays de la magie* (Paris: Gallimard, 1942); "In the Land of Magic" (extracts), in Henri Michaux, *Selected Writings*, trans. Richard Ellmann (London: New Directions, 1968), 237–70. I have sometimes modified the sections of Ellmann's translation that are used here.
2. Francis Ponge, *Le parti pris des choses* (Paris: Gallimard, 1942); *The Nature of Things*, trans. Lee Fahnestock (New York: Red Dust, 1995). I have sometimes modified Fahnestock's translation.

GHOST STORY

1. Franz Hellens, *Nouvelles reálités fantastiques* (Brussels: Les Écrits, 1941).
2. E. M. Forster, *Aspects of the Novel* (London: Edward Arnold, 1927; reissued 1941).
3. Achim von Arnim, *Le vase d'or, Le violon de Crémone, Le chevalier Gluck*, trans. Jean Duren (Paris: Gallimard, 1942); *The Golden Pot and Other Tales*, trans. Ritchie Robertson (Oxford: Oxford University Press, 1992).
4. Dominique Rolin, *Les marais* (Paris: Denoël, 1942).

5. Jean Cocteau, *Les enfants terribles* (Paris: Grasset, 1929); *The Holy Terrors*, trans. Rosamund Lehmann (New York: New Directions, 1955).

6. Alain-Fournier, *Le grand Meaulnes* (Paris: Emile-Paul, 1913); trans. Frank Davison (London: Penguin, 1966).

A USER'S GUIDE TO MONTHERLANT

1. Henri de Montherlant, *La vie en forme de proue* (Paris: Grasset, 1942).

2. Henri de Montherlant, *Service inutile* (Paris: Grasset, 1935); Henri de Montherlant, *La rose de sable* (Paris: Gallimard, 1968). Montherlant published the first version of this novel privately in 1938, under the pseudonym François Lazerge and with the title *Mission providentielle* (Paris: Imprimerie Ramlot). He then published the first part under his own name in 1951, with the title *Histoire d'amour de 'La rose de sable'* (Paris: Éditions des Deux-Rives).

CONSIDERATIONS ON THE HERO

1. Jacques Benoist-Méchin, *Ce qui demeure* (Paris: Albin Michel, 1942).

2. Daniel-Rops, *Psichari* (Paris: Plon, 1942).

3. Georges Dumézil, *Horace et les Curiaces* (Paris: Gallimard, 1942).

4. Marie-Louise Sjoested, *Dieux et héros des Celtes* (Paris: Presse Universitaires de France, 1940); *Gods and Heroes of the Celts*, trans. Myles Dillon (London: Methuen, 1949).

5. Friedrich Nietzsche, *Ecce Homo*, trans. Walter Kaufmann (New York: Vintage Books, 1967), 7.

"THE FINEST ROMANTIC BOOK"

1. J. W. von Goethe and Bettina von Arnim, *Correspondance de Bettina et de Goethe*, trans. Jean Triomphe (Paris: Gallimard, 1942); *Goethe's Correspondence with a Child*, trans. Bettina von Arnim (London, 1837–39).

2. Achim von Arnim, *Contes bizarres* (Paris: Editions des Cahiers Libres, 1933).

THAT INFERNAL AFFAIR

1. Henri Guillemin, *Cette affaire infernale* (Paris: Plon, 1942).

VIGILS OF THE MIND

1. Part of the fourth paragraph of this article is included in "Alain's Thinking," *FP*, 305.

2. Alain, *Vigiles de l'esprit* (Paris: Gallimard, 1942).

3. Alain, *Éléments de philosophie* (Paris: Gallimard, 1940); see "La pensée d'Alain," *Journal des Débats*, September 11, 1941; translated as "Alain's Thinking."

4. Pierre Naville, *La psychologie, science du comportement* (Paris: Gallimard, 1942).

5. John B. Watson, *Behaviourism* (London: Kegan Paul, Trench, Trubner & Co Ltd, 1925), 201.

FIRE, WATER, AND DREAMS

1. Gaston Bachelard, *L'intuition de l'instant* (Paris: Stock, 1932); *L'expérience de l'espace* (Paris: Alcan, 1937); *La philosophie du non. Essai d'une philosophie du nouvel esprit scientifique dans la physique contemporaine* (Paris: PUF, 1940); *The Philosophy of No: A Philosophy of the New Scientific Mind*, trans. G. C. Waterston (New York: Orion Press, 1968).

2. Gaston Bachelard, *L'eau et les rêves* (Paris: Corti, 1942); *Water and Dreams*, trans. Edith R. Farrell (Dallas: Pegasus Foundation, 1983); *La psychanalyse du feu* (Paris: Gallimard, 1938); *The Psychoanalysis of Fire*, trans. Alan C. M. Ross (London: Routledge & Kegan Paul, 1964).

3. Bachelard, *The Psychoanalysis of Fire*, 90.

4. Fragment 36. Clement of Alexandria, *Stromates*, VI, 17, 2.

5. Christopher Marlowe, *Doctor Faustus* (1604), Scene XIV.

6. Paul Éluard, "Pour vivre ici," in *Le livre ouvert I, 1938–40* (Paris: Éditions des Cahiers d'Art, 1940), 26.

7. Novalis, Maxim 1026, *Notes for a Romantic Encylopedia*, ed. David Wood (Albany, N.Y.: SUNY Press, 2007).

8. Edgar Allan Poe, "In the Maelstrom," *The Short Fiction of Edgar Allan Poe*, ed. Stuart Levine and Susan Levine (Champaign: University of Illinois Press, 1990), 41.

9. Bachelard, *Water and Dreams*, 214.

THE MEMORY OF MAUPASSANT

1. Paul Morand, *Vie de Guy de Maupassant* (Paris: Flammarion, 1942).

UNKNOWN ROMANTICS

1. Francis Dumont, *Naissance du romantisme contemporain* (Paris: Editions C.L., 1942).

2. André Breton, "Rabbe," *Minotaure* 10 (1936): 47.

3. See Gérard Bauër, *Les métamorphoses du romantisme* (Paris: Cahiers de la Quinzaine, 1928).

4. See "Unknown or Underrated Authors," *Into Disaster*.

5. Alphonse Rabbe, *L'album d'un pessimiste*, ed. Jules Marsan (Paris: Les Presses Françaises, 1924); Louis Andrieux, *Alphonse Rabbe* (Paris: Librairie Le Feu Follet, 1927).

6. "Un rêve," cited in Eldon Kaye, *Xavier Forneret, dit 'l'homme noir'* (Geneva: Droz, 1971), 153.

7. Xavier Forneret, "Un rêve," "Diamant de l'herbe," "Et la lune donnait et la rosée tombait," "Un oeil entre deux yeux," in *Contes et récits* (Paris: Corti, 1994).

REFUGES BY LÉON-PAUL FARGUE

1. Léon-Paul Fargue, *Le piéton de Paris* (Paris: Gallimard, 1939).

2. Léon-Paul Fargue, *Refuges* (Paris: Émile-Paul, 1942); *Déjeuners de soleil* (Paris: Gallimard, 1942).

3. This is a mistake, of course. It was Louis Aragon who made the remark in *Le paysan de Paris* (1926). See *The Paris Peasant*, trans. Simon Watson-Taylor (London: Jonathan Cape, 1971), 66–67. It is

interesting to speculate about whether this error was deliberate, and if so, why.

POETIC WORKS

1. Paul Éluard, *Poésie involontaire et poésie intentionnelle* (Villeneuve-lès-Avignon: Pierre Seghers, 1942); "Involuntary Poetry and Intentional Poetry," in Paul Éluard, *Shadows and Sun/Ombres et Soleil: Poems and Prose (1913–1952)*, trans. Cicely Buckley (Durham, N.C.: Oyster River Press, 1995).

2. The next four paragraphs from the original article form the chapter of *Faux pas* entitled "Involuntary Poetry."

3. Pierre Emmanuel, *Orphiques* (Paris: Gallimard, 1942).

4. Pierre Emmanuel, *Oeuvres completes, I* (Lausanne: L'Âge d'Homme, 2001), 1122.

5. Eugène Guillevic, *Terraqué* (Paris: Gallimard, 1942).

6. This is clearly a reference to Francis Ponge's *Le parti pris des choses* (*The Voice of Things*), which appeared in 1942. See "In the Land of Magic," this volume.

7. The original text in both the *Débats* and *Chroniques littéraires* erroneously has "Emmanuel's."

8. Claude Roy, *L'enfance de l'art* (Alger: Fontaine, 1942).

9. Maurice Fombeure, *À dos d'oiseau* (Paris: Gallimard, 1942).

BAD THOUGHTS BY PAUL VALÉRY

1. Paul Valéry, *Variétés I* (Paris: Gallimard, 1924).

2. Paul Valéry, *Mauvaises pensées et autres* (Paris: Gallimard, 1942); *Bad Thoughts and Not So Bad*, in *Analects*, trans. Stuart Gilbert, in *Collected Works of Paul Valéry*, ed. Jackson Mathews (Princeton: Princeton University Press, 1970), vol. 14:76.

3. Paul Valéry, *Analectes* (Paris: Gallimard, 1935); *Rhumbs* (Paris: Gallimard, 1933); *Choses tues* (Paris: Lapina, 1930). See *Collected Works of Paul Valéry*, ed. Jackson Mathews (Princeton: Princeton University Press, 1970), vol. 7.

4. Paul Valéry, *Introduction à la méthode de Léonard de Vinci* (Paris: Éditions de la Nouvelle Revue française, 1929); *Introduction*

to the Method of Leonardo da Vinci, trans. Thomas McGreevy (London: Rodker, 1929).

NEW NOVELS

1. Georges Magnane, *Les hommes forts* (Paris: Gallimard, 1942).
2. Marius Grout, *Le vent se lève* (Paris: Gallimard, 1942).
3. Marius Grout, *Musique d'avent* (Paris: Gallimard, 1941).
4. Maurice Toesca, *Clément* (Paris: Gallimard, 1942).
5. Roger de Lafforest, *Si le ciel tombe* (Paris: Éditions Colbert, 1942).

FROM TAINE TO M. DE PESQUIDOUX

1. Saint-René Taillandier, *Mon oncle Taine* (Paris: Plon, 1942).
2. Joseph de Pesquidoux, *Sol français* (Paris: Plon, 1942); *Chez nous* (Paris: Plon, 1921); *Sur la glèbe* (Paris: Plon, 1922); *Le livre de raison* (Paris: Plon, 1925–32).

Index